EVERY DAY ENERGY

EVERY DAY ENERGY

Using Meditation, Intuition and Clairvoyance in Your Life

BY ELIZABETH GUILBEAULT
EDITED BY F.J. LEE

Special thanks to my family and friends who cheered me along the way, especially those who took the time to read early editions and offer feedback. To my parents who bought me a typewriter that I had to have in order to write my first book back in 4th grade because real writers write on typewriters. To Nick, thank you for seeing me. To Paige, Samantha, Edith, Brighton, Josh and Roya, no words for all you have done for me. To my brothers who were my first meditation and energy teachers, thank you. To The Board, thank you for the energetic help to clear the way. To Robyn, thank you for urging me to keep going and highlighting points to include. To Faye, we did it!

About the Author

Elizabeth Guilbeault's most favorite thing to do is spend time with family and friends. She is the first to welcome you to visit and the last to leave a dinner table. As a student at heart, she loves reading (energy and books). Meditation and energy work changed her life and sharing that gift with others is her happy place. She has studied with many teachers and taken many classes throughout the years studying energy, meditation and yoga. This book is the result of those studies as well as the insights gained from her own practice and hours spent meditating and reading energy. When not sitting in her favorite chair meditating or giving readings, she enjoys laughing, hanging out and walking - each all the more when with family and friends. She thinks of herself as a good person with a sense of humor. She wrote this book primarily for her children to one day look back and understand what she was doing for all those hours in a chair with her eyes closed during their childhood.

CONTENTS

INTRODUCTION

MEDITATE. SEE. KNOW. TRUST. REPEAT.

If you read or hear the word, "elephant," what happens next?

Did Daisy, a flesh and tusk elephant from your local zoo, instantaneously materialize in sight and sound? Or, in your mind's eye did you see and hear an elephant proudly swinging his trunk, trumpeting loudly at a watering hole on the Serengeti? Perhaps an elephant from a long forgotten drawing you made as a child popped up. You can recall each crease of the paper and pinpoint exactly where you were when you drew it into being. Maybe the word elephant began typing across a dark screen in the recess of your mind with the clickity clack of a typewriter's keystrokes. You may have even felt the emotions elephants inspire for you—fear, love, strength or majesty. Heartache could have easily washed over you too if an orphaned Dumbo, in vivid Technicolor, newly separated from his mother, flew into view.

Why do I ask? To show you, we all, without effort, have the ability to intuitively and instantaneously think in pictures, sound and emotions, which are unique to us.

Intuition guides us in many ways. It is our ingrained sense of knowing, a hunch about what is or what will be that we cannot base in fact, only in deep, confident feeling. We all have intuition and we can all develop it more deeply—just as we can improve any skill like riding a bike, reading or being more compassionate towards others. With teaching and practice, in meditation, we can hone our intuitive abilities to better access the energy and information flowing around, within and between us.

Meditation is mainstream now. It is prescribed by medical doctors for anxiety, incorporated into employee wellness programs and taught in elementary schools. The benefits of meditation for calming and de-stressing are scientifically accepted, and anyone can do it. The energy-focused practice I teach in Everyday Energy amplifies traditional meditation's deep relaxation benefits while integrating intuition development to increase self-knowledge and strengthen our connection to our authentic selves. It also provides a more enlivened meditation session for those who find their focus wanes, or their eyes get too sleepy with a quieter, repetitive practice.

When we intentionally tap into energy in meditation guided by our intuition, pictures, sounds, and feelings appear to us as effortlessly and as real as our elephants. As an energy practitioner and healer, I have been taught—and have experienced firsthand—that the images, emotions and sensations that emerge in meditation hold real meaning. They contain messages to enlighten and guide us towards truth and healing. We only need to figure out how to interpret them.

In the pages that follow, you will learn how to know, see and clear energy in meditation as well as how to recognize and develop your own intuitive gifts. Our practice integrates body, mind and spirit. It at once centers and relaxes us while promoting healing and growth by helping us make sense of the energy we experience every day.

I can attest that reading energy and working with your intuition in meditation is truly as simple as:

Meditate. See. Know. Trust. Repeat.

Meditation and energy work are my passion. I came here to learn it, teach it and grow with it. It is my sincere pleasure to share this meditation and energy work space with you. Throughout the pages that follow I seek to introduce you to techniques, ideas, and meditations to help you develop your practice, grow your ability to intuit and see, and trust what you energetically feel and see. Meditation is an avenue to develop your intuition, which can serve you every day in your life, providing insights, knowledge and guidance.

We all have the ability to incorporate meditation and intuition into our daily lives. We only need to give it a whirl and, as with any skill, practice. Let's jump in and get started. Suspend your disbelief, mute society's programming and follow me with your curiosity—or might it be your intuition?

Chapter 1: Getting to Know Energy

Energy is best described as the unseen vibrations encircling us all the time. Everything is energy. It is everywhere, every day, all the time, in different forms and always changing. It is neither created nor destroyed. It simply is. It is powerful. It is dynamic. It flows within us and swirls around us much like water in a tide pool. We can resist it and avoid it, never knowing what could have been. Or we can embrace it and follow to see where it takes us. We can also read it and see beyond what meets the eye of our consciousness.

We all intuitively read energy in our daily lives even if we are unaware or frame it in different terms. We tune in to energy consciously and unconsciously throughout our days and nights. Consciously, we witness a tender moment between a parent and child and instantly feel uplifted, or we inadvertently overhear neighbors arguing and it leaves us with uneasiness for hours. In witnessing such moments, we often unconsciously match to the energy of the exchanges.

Meditation helps reveal our conscious and unconscious responses to energies we encounter. When we are aware, we can be better gatekeepers for ourselves in choosing which energies we allow in as well as those we release into the world. One of the first steps we take in meditation and energy work to further develop our intuitive abilities is to work on being present and mindful. We can then move, with practice, to quickly identify when sudden shifts in our emotional planes occur and press pause to take a look. This gives us the awareness, space and time to choose how to respond, instead of automatically taking on new energies that circle near, and reacting.

Another way we intuitively read energy without being fully aware is through gut feelings. We can all likely recount a time this type of "knowing" happened to us. We had unshakable faith in its validity despite not being able to explain it. Maybe we uncharacteristically hesitated about going to a party we had been looking forward to all week moments before it began. We felt something was off on a visceral, emotional level and possibly even experienced a distressing physical response when we reached for our car keys. The clear message being "don't go," yet we had no reason to skip the party.

When we heed these intuitive feelings and make a course correction, we feel relief and peace. We know in the seat of our soul it is the right call. We rarely linger on the why. We go on with our lives and tuck these unnerving, unexplainable experiences away because they may make us feel self-conscious or maybe even irrational. We fear the judgment of others in our lives and even inside our own families. Will they look down upon us as superstitious or absurd or worse?

Love is one of the most powerful forces in nature. If we are lucky, we will experience it deeply and often at many points in our lives—as a child, parent, grandparent, partner, friend, pet owner and more. Despite its undeniable existence and strong imprint on our human lives, we can neither see it nor hold it in our hands. There is no question it is real and consequential. More practically, we know Wi-Fi abounds in our homes and communities; yet cannot detect it with our five senses alone. We cannot see our text ping from iPhone to satellite tower to our friend's Apple watch miles away, but it arrives all the same. Also, pause for a second to imagine traveling back in time to explain such a phenomenon to your great grandparents. Invisible what? Traveling through the air? On mini pocket phones and watches without wires? It would sound preposterous, right? What if the energies I describe, traveling through and around us, are just as real as love or Wi-Fi, yet still undetectable—except to the intuitively woke?

There are religious traditions and medical practices centuries old in many corners of our world that believe in the existence of various types of life energies imbuing our world and us. Acupuncture and traditional Chinese medicine believe there is chi flowing through energy meridians in our body. Many have heard the word chakra, meaning energy center in the body, at some point in their life. These energetic concepts continue to gain traction in mainstream culture.

I encourage all newcomers to meditation to hold space for what may seem like a far-out type of mediation practice at first. Resist the want to dismiss it because it feels too woo-woo or unfamiliar. Our western society has programmed us to react this way and to ignore knowledge that has cut across cultures and world religions for millennia. I invite you to push past fear and disbelief as you begin or move further into your own journey into meditation, intuition and energy work. Use your practice to notice what happens, to explore new insights, and to see beyond what you might have otherwise normally seen. It can be as effortless and natural as calling forth your elephant. If we can clear the trepidation and give ourselves permission to open up, even momentarily, we can experience insight and peace in meditation and energy work, and, perhaps, connect with the intuitive knowledge that our existence holds much more than meets the eye.

Reading Energy for Yourself

In the process of becoming an energy worker and healer, I cultivated my awareness of energy and my own intuition through practicing meditation and seeing energy. Through incorporating meditation techniques that I learned from many generous teachers along the way into my daily life, I learned to identify, run and read energy as well as how to develop my intuition to contextually interpret what I saw, heard and felt in meditation. I have practiced asking questions (What is going on? What is the energy of this situation? What is the picture associated with this energy?) in meditation to the point that now the curiosity that sparks the questions is ever present in my body, mind and spirit. When emotions or sensations come on quickly like a title wave or when gut feelings pop up out of the blue, my first inclination is to look at a picture of the energy and investigate. Information on the "what" is always found in the energy of the event, meeting or individual. Tuning in, seeing and reading energy in meditation unlocks this for us.

Some may wonder if this is a tool to figure out others' information. While that is possible to an extent, it is more so about seeing our own information and understanding our personal growth, changes and life path. It is about gaining high-level insight into our purpose in this lifetime and stripping back the external layers to connect more deeply to our own spirit, or authentic self. I have also come to use this ability in readings for others, and you may find you are called to do the same. However, the power, for me, continues to lie in the ability to notice, see, know and have my information and my answers.

In meditation, through receiving messages via pictures, sounds and/or emotions, we gain a better understanding of the issue at hand and how it relates to us and our current path. For example, when we tune-in and see a picture associated with the energy we feel—the unspoken or unconscious vibe we picked up on—it helps everything make more sense. Once you can see something, you can understand it, decide if you want to embrace it or clear it in meditation through various energetic methods (more on that shortly) and take the next step on your path. Tapping into this intuitive understanding brings deep healing. The more we practice meditation and reading energy, the easier it becomes. The more we tune in, the more connected we feel to ourselves and our energy.

With time and practice, you might find you are able to immediately transition into meditation whenever you would like to tune in. You may not need to be in deep, contemplative meditation mode. Maybe you are on a jog, in line at the DMV or on a conference call when a picture flashes from your mind's eye. As you practice, the better and faster you get at centering, seeing, having your information and reading energy clearly every day no matter where you find yourself or how little time you have to meditate.

For me, practicing meditation and looking at the energy of situations, people, things and, basically, all of life, continues to help me make sense of what is before me, provides guidance and, perhaps most beneficially, eases my anxiety and stress. Reading energy propels me into deep relaxation and consciously demystifies events happening around me. It has allowed me to find joy in the parts of the tide pool of life I had not wanted to fully embrace before meditation came into my life. Seeing and reading energy has fostered an ability to embrace the unexpected, to recognize signs and symbols as they materialize and to trust what is unfolding even when I may not feel ready at the moment.

Shortly after giving birth to my third daughter, a nurse came into my hospital room to check on me. She mentioned that it was her son's twenty-first birthday, the son she had after having three daughters. As she smiled at me, I had an inkling she was there to give me a message along the lines of "you too might find yourself having your fourth and it being a boy one day." I looked at her and smiled back thinking "I love that you have four children and you got the boy, however, I am not ready to hear your message!"

About six months later, while sitting in meditation, I saw three girls running through my kitchen followed by a little boy. His name in the meditation was Brighton. I knew instantly that he was my son and that we would, in fact, have four biological children. I couldn't help but think of the nurse and send an energetic thank you to her for helping to open the gate for me to see this picture. Initially after giving birth to my third, I wasn't feeling particularly keen on the idea of doing the whole pregnancy thing again. When it was time, I was ready, and a little over two years after my third daughter was born, we did welcome a son into the world. We kept the name he showed me in meditation, a name I only knew through that meditation.

Then, we received the most amazing wink from the Universe. When I was about five months pregnant, my middle daughter who was three at the time, came to me and said she knew the name of her soon to be brother. While my husband and I knew the name, she did not. We hadn't told a soul. She said very confidently "his name is something like Shiny." A name like Brighton can't get much closer to Shiny if you ask me.

My fourth child represents an experience where I read the energy for myself. I received the messages sent to me and opened myself up in meditation to seeing my next steps. Then I let them unfold. I used my meditation practice to guide me in the steps to take, while simultaneously detaching from knowing exactly how, when and what. There is no way to predict for sure you will have a boy or girl. If he had ended up being a girl, we would have welcomed her and not missed a beat. Meditating, intuiting, and seeing is not about controlling the outcome, but rather opening up to receiving the insights along your path to ease the steps ahead. Having a fourth baby could have been overwhelming, surprising and intense. The heads up from the information and pictures I intuited along the way made welcoming another child a much gentler process than it could have been otherwise.

Meditation and intuition help ease growth and next steps, giving you an opportunity to have insight into the possibilities of what is to come. It is not about predicting the future perfectly or always knowing exactly what will unfold. It is about tuning in to the possibilities and being open to the present moment to have the experiences reveal themselves to you. When you practice meditating and tuning in to your intuition, you get to know your pictures and start recognizing your answers for yourself. To know yourself, your pictures, your information is powerful.

Reading Energy for Others

In time, meditation and energy practitioners may feel called to help others read and clear their energy, which is healing for the reader as well as for the person receiving the reading. Energy workers/healers usually practice tuning in and understanding the information they receive by first having clarity about themselves (accomplished using meditation) before moving to assist others. Then, with practice, they feel ready to read the energy of others or teach them how to access their own answers via meditation.

For me, it felt like a natural evolution to transition into an energy reader and healer. I would never have predicted this calling as a child and certainly not as a young adult pursuing a degree in finance. I did not recognize my intuitive abilities for what they were as a young girl, and the household I grew up in did not talk in those terms. I learned to ignore or mislabel this side of myself for years as a result. Rather than calling it intuition, I would call it a coincidence when things came together as I had intuited them. I would marvel at how something happened to work out, even though I had felt called to act on certain events in particular ways based on gut feelings or impulses.

It wouldn't be until a family reunion in my late teens where a cousin who practiced astrology would imply that I too could develop my intuition and be an energy worker. Her suggestion gave me pause and unlocked my curiosity. Although I felt unsure what to do with this information, I would reflect upon our conversation multiple times over the next several years. Eventually the opportunity would arise to take yoga and meditation classes with a friend. I felt at home immediately. The classes reawakened my intuition and introduced me to meditation techniques that would help me develop my abilities further.

I remember a fellow student in my early days of learning and practicing meditation and energy work saying to me during a reading that I could teach this and help others to develop their intuitive abilities. At the time, that picture did not resonate with me. I wanted the information to use to find my own answers and have clarity in my own life. Sometimes we aren't ready to have the information others share with us. We receive insights to tuck away and revisit at a later time.

Yoga helped me find a greater awareness of my body while meditation helped me connect to my thoughts, feelings and the energies around and within me. The more I practiced yoga and meditated, the more I noticed what was my energy and what was not my energy. Meditation created a place for me to release what did not belong to me in order to work with and understand what was authentically mine. We all have a unique vibration, our own frequency, and our own energy. Meditation fosters a connection with this energy, creating a channel to our true selves. When you are connected to your own unique vibration, it becomes easier to create the life you want. The more tuned in you are to your energy, the easier to connect to your body, mind and spirit which in turn lends itself to ensuring you are on your path instead of someone else's or one that has been constructed for you.

As many of us have likely experienced in life and it is the same in meditation, you cannot solve what is not yours. If you attempt to fix problems that you do not own, you will spin your wheels or experience a forceful reaction to your intervention. On the contrary, if you undertake figuring out a personal challenge, it is much easier to navigate, find answers and take next steps. When reading for others, it is not my job to take on or solve the challenges in front of the person. Rather, in intuiting, seeing, and reading for someone else, I am offering a neutral perspective of the energies in the person's body and space (meaning a designated area around the body, for these purposes, about two to three feet 360 degrees around a person) and sharing the insights presented for them to take as their own to resolve, understand and move forward in their life on their journey.

When I sit to do a reading, I first get centered through meditation to ensure that I am present and showing up for the reading. I check that I am grounded and ready to see from a neutral place (the center of my head). As I have practiced over the years, this process has gotten faster and faster as I have gotten quicker at knowing my energy, what it looks like and what it feels like, ensuring I am reading from a neutral place. Then, while in meditation, I read the pictures that pop up when questions from the person receiving the reading are asked. As a practiced reader and healer, it is not an energy drain to read for someone (often it is energizing). I have created a place in meditation from my mind's eye to read and see pictures as they pop up. The question from the person prompts the pictures. As the reading unfolds, the pictures morph and change as new questions arise. Since it is not my information, I usually don't remember a lot of the specifics or the pictures that pop up in a reading. I relay the pictures and information for the person to receive, then let them go.

During a reading, I am mindful not to take on the client's energy, as I have practiced meditation techniques that have taught me to know my energy, what it looks like and feels like. However, I am human with faults and am still susceptible to taking on other people's energy in day-to-day activities, especially when not paying attention as the busy-ness of life takes over some days. When I do find myself taking on someone's energy unconsciously, I usually notice it relatively quickly because I have practiced knowing my energy. When dropping something off to a friend one time, I noticed that I felt jittery when I got back in the car. I had felt fine on my way to meet the person, yet after talking and visiting with the person for a bit, then getting back in my car, something shifted. I started driving and by the time I got home, I knew I had taken on some of my friend's energy. Her energy in my space felt uneasy, jumpy, and not like mine. I felt off and, lucky for me, I live in a house of energy workers, when I came in the door and mentioned to my husband I felt off, unsettled and restless, he chimed in that it looked like I had taken on some of the friend's energy. With a quick grounding and a few deep breaths, I felt back to myself again and carried on with my day. It was a great reminder to me of how quickly we can take on someone else's energy. Note that my friend's energy wasn't necessarily jittery in her space because it belonged to her. It showed up in my space as feelings of unease because it wasn't mine. When it isn't our energy, it usually doesn't fit well in our space. No real harm would have come if I hadn't grounded right away and cleared out the energy that wasn't mine, as it would have eventually cleared out some other way. Recognizing it early on made it easier to clear out and get on with my day and my to do list the way that felt best for me without managing through energy that didn't fit me.

Using meditation techniques to tune in to your intuition and the energy of those around you does not mean that you walk around reading others all the time. Although as family and friends discover your growing ability, you may find yourself fielding inquiries as to whether or not you are reading them every time you see them. My experience is that we all have too much going on for ourselves to spend our time reading others everywhere we go. As you get quicker and quicker at accessing your intuition and seeing your pictures, you can certainly pop into the space of reading yourself and others more and more quickly, however, that doesn't mean reading everyone everywhere you go. You have ownership over how your intuition works in your life. You get to decide how and when you access your meditation, intuition and clairvoyance.

As you move through the techniques, stories and meditations in this book, you may decide your goal is to read energy for others as well as yourself. Alternatively, you may decide the information is for you to develop your meditation practice and intuitive language for yourself solely. There is no right or wrong when it comes to meditation and energy work. The information presented allows you to validate your intuition, your insights and your abilities to see beyond the physical as well as fosters your body, mind and spirit connection in ways that deepen your understanding of yourself and others to bring you to a new level of peace, love and joy in your life and on your path every day.

Chapter 2: Meditation Basics

When a friend, student or client feels stuck, one of the first things I suggest is to meditate, ground and be in their energy. In particular, I recommend sitting with the issue at hand in meditation to see what thoughts, feelings or pictures surface. Sitting in a space of quiet reflection offers a pathway to clarity when answers feel elusive.

There are many ways to meditate. I encourage clients to do what feels best and make it work for them. There are an infinite variety of ways to work with energy, too. I will touch on several meditation strategies as well as clearing energy strategies to build a practice that lends itself to developing your intuition as well as seeing and working with energy. Then, it is up to you to take what resonates, play with meditation in your life and let the techniques become yours to use every day. In my own life, I practice these techniques daily. I work with energy every day. One of my mantras is every day energy. I consciously practice and notice energy in my life every day. The more you practice and play with the techniques, the easier to access them when you need them the most. Let them become a daily habit as you open up to accessing your intuition and clairvoyance through meditation.

Grounding Cords Aren't Only for Trees

Using a tool called a grounding cord in meditation creates a way to visualize releasing, or letting go, of energy we want to clear. I discovered this technique early in my meditation journey. It tunes us in, connects us with our bodies, minds and spirits and moves energy. It changed everything for me.

For years, people had said to me "let it go." It sounded easy enough. Yet for me, until I learned the technique of grounding, letting go seemed at times overwhelming. Once I experienced grounding, I looked forward to meditating and working with my grounding cord daily. I went from trying to meditate by "clearing" my head, or consciously working hard to think of nothing, to the reverse—actively meditating on pressing issues and visually shedding unwanted energy via my grounding cord. I instantly felt my body relax, my shoulders release and my stresses ease with the healing grounding permits.

With the right techniques, meditation can feel easy. A grounding cord gives a focal point and provides an avenue to release energy you might carry that does not belong to you or anything you feel ready to let go of from your day, week, month, year or lifetime (past or present). A grounding cord is a visual aid to represent the concept of letting go. When you ground, tuning in to how you feel in meditation becomes easier and clearer. Grounding affords us the opportunity to check in and pay attention to our bodies. We are brought into our bodies, to present time, when we ground.

To practice meditation and work with a grounding cord, imagine a cord dropping from the base of your spine, at the tailbone, and connecting you to the center of the Earth. Feel free to visualize any image as your grounding cord — a line of color, a waterfall, a rope, a blade of grass, a rainbow, a tree trunk, a stem of a rose, any visual. Play around. Change it up. The key is to make it feel good to you and to feel its support. Then, let the issue, blockage, and energy of the situation run out and down our grounding cord into the Earth's core. It is a simple, yet effective technique that will serve you in your meditation practice.

A grounding cord is one way we can choose to ground, release and connect ourselves to the Earth and feel its support. We have likely experienced grounding, though we may not have called it that, at other times in our lives. For example, while in nature, we may have felt connected to the Earth. Perhaps we were jogging outdoors, gardening, playing in the sand at the beach, walking barefoot on a summer day, camping under the stars or making a snow angel when we felt rooted and connected. Anytime we connect to the Earth, emotionally and/or physically, we ground our energy, ourselves and, in turn, feel one with the natural world.

Excursions into the outdoors are known and accepted by cultures all over the globe as a way to center and rejuvenate. We find peace and healing in nature that we cannot muster in the hustle and bustle of our modern lives alone. Spending time outdoors away from our normal existences provides peace, healing and a reset. It is not surprising that "forest bathing" has appealed as a valid way to de-stress and rejuvenate. We yearn to eat lunch outdoors and feel the sunshine on our faces if only for a few minutes. We bring the natural world indoors as much as we can with plants, botanical materials, photos of natural environments, expansive landscape paintings and essential oils that invoke a blooming rose garden, salty beach air or a grove of lemon trees.

After completing my first marathon in 2003, I realized that running was grounding. I trained for the Chicago marathon over many months, and at first, not being a lifelong runner, I didn't quite understand the whole running culture and why people were such devotees. Afterwards, I understood why runners became addicted and I even felt the "runner's high" myself. It all felt oddly familiar, and it dawned on me that what I experienced on training run after training run was what I experienced in meditation. When sitting in meditation with a grounding cord releasing energy, I created space for my body to let things go. I felt peace and in the flow as well as supported by the Earth. While running, the repetition of my feet connecting with the pavement grounded me to the Earth and allowed me to shed energy not serving me. I was training my body to run while also creating an energetic channel to release energy, thoughts, worries and concerns down to the Earth through grounding with each stride.

All the training in preparation for the race gave me time to ground on a regular basis. I released, cleared, and let go of a lot. As I unconsciously sent stress, worries, fears and who knows what else away through the soles of my feet, I created space for new energies to surface. While I did not directly correlate the running to grounding until months went by, the feeling of ease and lightness of being was unmistakable. Now I completely understand what runners mean when they talk about the clarity they get after a long outdoor run - not only from experiencing it on the physical level - from an energetic perspective as well. Energetically, when you run, you are grounding – releasing and clearing energy every time your foot connects to the Earth. Each step helps you physically, mentally and emotionally discard things that may be cluttering your body, mind, and spirit, giving you the opportunity to experience increased clarity and insight into your life.

Much like a run helps us clear our heads, find focus and release stress and tension, a grounding cord offers the same type of support to the body, albeit a little gentler on the hips and knees. We often use going for a run or walk as an escape to release the background noise from our day - the tensions at the office, the stress at home. We can then connect more fully with our thoughts, listen to our feelings, strengthen our bodies and reset ourselves. Through meditating and practicing working with the image of a grounding cord, I discovered how to get many of the same healing benefits without having to lace up my running shoes.

Grounding provides a tremendous healing, either with an energetic grounding cord or with a physical connection to the Earth. It creates an opportunity to merge ourselves - body, mind and spirit - with nature while releasing, clearing and letting go of energies that no longer serve our highest and best selves. When you are grounded, you are acutely aware of your actions, live in the moment and stay present in your body. Whether physically (by actions connecting us to the Earth) or energetically (through visual aids and intention in meditation), we create a connection between the natural world and ourselves when we ground.

Grounding as a meditation technique brings us into our bodies and into present time, much like physical outdoor activities. It is a tool that can be used every day, anytime and anywhere. Grounding is especially helpful when we lack the time to run, walk or garden. We can practice it with our eyes closed or open, while safely sitting, standing, walking or working. With it, we find focus, clarity, and insight while simultaneously finding an avenue to release energies we are done with that inhabit our space.

I benefited greatly from the clearing my training for the marathon offered without even realizing it. Now, I do not run nearly as much as I did then. Instead, I practice grounding every day, usually multiple times a day, both in meditation and when moving through my day. When I forget to use a grounding cord, things feel stuck. While a grounding cord does not replace running, it can be a great addition to your workouts, your meditation practice and your daily routine in general. Every time you ground, every time you connect to your body in the present moment, it is a healing for you as it creates space for you to tune in to your body, mind and spirit and connect to your energy. When you connect to your energy, it is much easier to know your truth, to have your answers, to know what you want and what you need, as well as to feel good, safe and comfortable in your body. Your body was designed for you - was made for you - and works best when you are present in it. Grounding helps you have that experience.

Bubbles Aren't Only for Popping

We all pick things up – physically and energetically—throughout our days. Physically, it is easy to see. We grab that extra cookie from the lunch buffet. We walk by a jacket on a chair and hang it in the coat closet. We pick up a quarter on the sidewalk and tuck it in our pocket. Energetically though, we do not always realize what we acquire as we navigate our day.

We go to work. Our co-worker is feeling upset. We sit down to work in the adjoining cubical and gradually feel upset by the end of the day without realizing why. On the drive home, we stop at the pharmacy still carrying that energy with us and spread it to three other people we encounter in the aisles. At the checkout counter, the cashier is in a cheerful mood. Without realizing it, we absorb this happy energy, which cancels out the unpleasant energy we had been lugging about all day. We resume our drive home lighter and with a smile on our face not fully comprehending what occurred. We instead focus on what to have for dinner, a looming deadline or a show we cannot wait to get in our pajamas to watch.

As we explored, grounding gives us a chance to release what we might not even realize we are holding onto such as the energy of others that we allow consciously and unconsciously to enter our space. Another technique to add to our toolbox to keep our energy in and other energies out is a protection bubble. Children in particular love this technique as they can picture themselves in giant soap bubbles they blow in the park.

Imagine if you had a bubble surrounding you everywhere you went. How would it feel to have a space that belongs only to you? You can bring it closer or expand it as needed. If you want a little more space at work or at home, expand your bubble. Feeling snuggly with your family or pet on the couch while watching a movie, bring your bubble closer to you.

The technique of a bubble around you gives you a visual of a protected space around your body (usually about two to three feet in circumference) that acts like a filter and boundary. It is like the walls of a house. In a house, you open a door or window to let people and objects in and out much like you can expand or constrict your bubble to allow movement in the space around your body or not. Without the walls, doors and windows, a house might feel exposed, drafty and not very safe. Your bubble acts like walls, doors and windows, giving you comfort, security and the ability to decide what energies come in and out of your space. You can play with the images you use as protection as well. Some of my clients use a line of hedges to define their space. Others have created different color rings around their body and space. Sometimes the protection image you use changes. Be creative and flexible as you get comfortable with what works for you in your meditation.

Ideally, protecting your space doesn't come from a place of fear, rather it flows from a place of empowerment. You get to decide how your space feels for you. With the visual or intention of a protection bubble around your body defining your space (imagine standing in the middle of a bubble or standing still and drawing a chalk circle around yourself), you get to filter out what energies you don't want coming into your space. Likewise, you can fill your space with the energies you do want. You can imagine peace, love, abundance, joy or laughter (or a combination of them all) raining down inside your bubble. As you play with the different energies, you can notice what they feel like and what you enjoy having in your space. When other energies come in as they do since this is not a perfect system (we are all human, interacting with others so sharing energy is part of the experience), you can notice them and ground them out if desired and then refill your bubble with the energy you would like to have in your space.

In our bodies, we have multiple systems, complex organs and neurons firing in complicated networks of communication to keep our physical selves humming along. When something goes awry, our body sends messages via a stomachache, a pain in the tooth or a fever. Those signal to us that something is amiss. Our energetic system doesn't always trigger responses as fine tuned as our body systems have developed, mostly because we don't practice them every day. We feel something or notice something, yet we aren't sure. We doubt ourselves, and we ignore it. It eventually gets stronger and moves into the body where we can't ignore it any longer. That thought that you needed to see the dentist has moved from a possibility to an urgent situation as your tooth is aching in severe pain. Why didn't we listen when we felt the first inkling?

If your space is full of noise from other people, it's easy to miss messages. When you work with a protection bubble, you create space to have more of your energy and information at hand making it easier to recognize insights about what is happening for you. In a perfect system, you would recognize the toothache before it became a ten on the pain scale.

In taking a few moments daily to ground and set your space with a protection bubble around it, you foster communication between your body and your energy. You are setting up a filter to avoid accumulating other people's energy in your space while also keeping your energy wrapped in your own space. Other people's energy in our own spaces clouds our ability to receive our own intuitive messages, especially as they relate to our bodies. Your energy works best for you and mine for me. When your energy is in your body and space, you set yourself up to receive the messages when they are more gentle like a whisper instead of a scream to get your attention.

Have you ever noticed yourself trying to do something the way someone else does it and it doesn't work for you no matter how you try? We aren't designed to be carbon copies of each other. We each have our own unique vibration and way of existing. When we are aligned with our own way of doing things, more often than not, we experience ease. In teaching my children how to tie their shoes, I have observed this exact concept. I showed them how to tie shoes, then each of my children had to take their own shoes and practice to find their own variation that worked for them. I taught them the basics and then they had to find their style, tightness and decide whether to tie a single or double knot. This is an example of learning a technique and adapting it to work for you. We all tie our shoes. The exact way we tie them, looks different and feels different. That is energy. We all have it and when we own ours, we are better able to connect with our path, our purpose and our direction in life. When we tie our shoes the way we like them, we walk taller, run faster and feel better.

Practice working with this idea of having a protection bubble around your space and notice how your energy shifts, your body feels, and if you are able to tune in faster to your intuitive messages. Let the image of a protection bubble work for you – get creative! You can make it to your liking. See it as a clear bubble or choose different colors or maybe even select different images (some of my clients have said they prefer the image of hedges lining the edge of their space). Set your space up so that it allows maximum comfort for you. Allow yourself to change things up as you see fit. Your protection bubble will morph as your energy shifts and changes. Keep it fresh and let yourself have fun creating a space that is fitting to you and your unique vibration.

Your Energy Isn't Only for Looking Pretty

In addition to grounding and protecting ourselves from outside energies, practicing having our own, unique energy vibration kicks what does not belong to us out of our space. Empty places want to be filled. If you move to a house with three bedrooms, you find ways to utilize them. The energetic space around your body, as well as your body, is like those bedrooms. It wants to be filled. It can be full of other people's energy or full of your own energy. We each have our own unique energy, our own vibration. When we fill our body and our space with our energy, we maximize our chance to be on our path and to connect to our life purpose.

If you have ever heard someone describe being in the zone or have been there yourself, this is an example of a time when you were fully engulfed in your energy. When we have our energy in our body and space, we are in the zone, in the flow; we feel confident and good. It's not that everything will go perfectly that we will not miss a shot or be immune from mistakes. Rather, it is being in a place of complete trust and knowing of what is unfolding. When we are in the zone, we are not full of questions or doubt; we are certain in our spot and move with that certainty and confidence. When you have your energy filling up your body and space, you create the conditions to experience that in the zone feeling. Your space is full of your energy. Your wishes and goals materialize because you created an opening to see and have your information. When we are full of energy and information that belongs to others, it makes it challenging to see our own desires and path ahead. The concept of using a visual to fill your body and space with your own energy becomes an invaluable technique to assist in manifesting and creating the life you desire.

The technique I like the most for helping my energy dominate my own space is imagining my own personal sun above my head shining down filling me with the warmth and glow that only a beautiful radiant sun provides. I visualize the golden light radiating off the sun shining down and filling my body and the space around my body with my unique energy. The best part is that the sun is constantly replenishing itself with the energy I share with the world as I move about my day. When I pause and imagine my sun shining down, it is automatically filling me back in with my energy that returns to me like a radiant boomerang. Your energy is the best healing to you. Visualizing and feeling your energy energizes and rejuvenates you.

Another way to visualize your energy filling your space is imagining your energy raining down on you. You can see it as different colors that may change day-to-day, hour-to-hour as your energy shifts and changes. Since we all see things differently, trust that the color that pops up for you when you set the intention to see your energy is your unique energy at that moment. As you meditate more, play with how your energy appears to you and what the different colors mean to you. Have fun by making it glitter or sparkle, shine and shimmer. There is no right or wrong way to work with your energy.

When I see my energy as a color, I like to lace it with my unique gold energy, whatever color goal appears to me. Gold is a higher vibrational color and energy, yet not quite as high of a vibration as the color or energy of white. Working with gold energy allows you to stay present in the body as you meditate and move through your day with your energy in your space while also offering you a healing because of the higher vibrational quality it has. White tends to pull us out of our bodies because of its high vibration. White covers all visible spectrums of color giving it the higher vibrational quality. I use gold when I work with energy throughout my day, as my aim is to stay present.

It bears repeating: your energy is the most healing energy for you. When you have your energy filling your body and space, it is a healing to you. When you are working with your energy, it is easier to see what you want to do, to create, and to have. Have you ever gone to a restaurant and they brought you someone else's meal instead of what you ordered? Most likely, you sent it back because it wasn't yours. When something is not ours, it usually doesn't work or feel right for us. We might be able to tolerate eating someone else's order every once in a while, yet on a regular basis, it won't do. We would feel increasingly frustrated or tired of not getting what we ordered. When you work with someone else's energy in your space, it's as if you are receiving someone else's meal all the time instead of your own.

On the contrary, when you fill your body and space with your energy, you open up the opportunity to tune in and create what you want. You are, in effect, lining up with your higher purpose. If you imagine the sun or the rain drops falling into your space as representing your energy filled with the essence of your higher purpose and let it flow down and around you, you are filling your space with your purpose, your calling, your energy.

I moved into an apartment with a roommate my junior year in college. It was then I noticed that about every other month, I would want to spend an entire weekend alone watching movies or doing whatever I wanted to do. I became aware that my energy felt zapped, leaving me feeling exhausted. It wasn't until I started meditating, releasing energy down my grounding cord and filling back in with my own energy that I made the connection. I didn't have the vocabulary to know then that I gave away my energy a little at a time and did not know to replenish it. It took about six to eight weeks and I would need a solid day or two to recharge my batteries. When I started meditating, I no longer needed that day or two of isolation to re-energize because I mindfully released and refueled during meditation. While I still enjoy a movie night or a rainy weekend of relaxing with my family on the couch, this solo recovery time has gone from being a necessity to being a luxury thanks to my tools. As I look back on those college days, I wish I had known about meditation and what these techniques could have afforded me then.

Meditation: Getting to Know Your Energy

For our first meditation, let's explore the three techniques: grounding, protection bubble and filling in with your own energy.

Once you are comfortable with this meditation, use it as a springboard and basis to move into the meditations that follow. Learning to know and recognize my energy before reading energy made sense in my development. As always, learn and explore them in the order that feels right for you. Anyone is welcome to jump ahead and start where they feel is best for them. Make it work for you. If it doesn't resonate with you, you won't want to build your own practice and incorporate the techniques into your every day life.

To begin, find a position and location that is both safe and comfortable for you. I often meditate sitting in a chair with my feet on the ground. This posture is known for aligning oneself energetically with the Earth and my body feels well supported while seated. Others may prefer lying down, standing or even walking (with eyes open for safety, of course). Trust whatever position you feel is best in the moment. Similarly, regarding location, meditate wherever you feel comfortable. Perhaps it is your porch swing, a comfy floor cushion, your parked car, the subway during your morning commute, your favorite recliner or all the above. Pick what feels right for you and keep in mind, you may want to change it up depending on the day, the weather and your mood.

Let's get started!

Settle into your body by taking a deep breath, inhaling and exhaling through your nose if that feels comfortable to you. Close your eyes or soften your gaze, letting your eyes drift toward the floor. Take an-

other inhale and exhale, lengthening the breath as you go. Continue to breathe throughout the meditation, inhaling and exhaling through the nose, noticing, if you begin to hold your breath at any point, and simply restart your breathing. You can come back to your breath anytime, anywhere. As you continue to breathe, send the message to your body giving permission to relax – roll the neck and shoulders, wrists and ankles, a few times – taking a moment to connect with your body. Send your breath all the way down to your toes as you inhale and as you exhale, give yourself permission to let go of anything you are ready to release.

On your next breath, give yourself a grounding cord. Visualize a charging cord, a beanstalk, a comet's tail, a piece of yarn, a line of color, a waterfall, a spider's strand of silk, whatever image pops up for you, from the base of your spine connecting you to the center of the Earth. There is no right or wrong. Whatever image pops up for you is perfect. Imagine the grounding cord connecting your body from the base of your spine all the way down to the center of the Earth. Tethering you to the Earth while also creating a channel for you to release anything you are ready to let go. As you breathe, expand your grounding cord out, widening it so that the grounding cord supports your entire body and some space around you. You are now grounded and connected to the Earth. Set the intention to release anything in your body or the space around you that you are ready to let go simply by telling yourself it is okay to do so. Notice how your body may shift, move, and feel. You might instantly feel lighter. You may notice your breath changing, your shoulders relaxing even more, and your attention shifting to different areas of your body or thoughts. As thoughts come up, let them. Acknowledge thoughts and feelings that surface. If your mind drifts to your to-do list, that's okay. You can come right back to meditation at any point. As you continue to ground, allow any images, words, or symbols that pop up, to be present in your space. You don't have to know or understand all that arises. Give yourself a chance to just observe and notice.

Grounding is a powerful technique to clear and release stress, tension and energy that doesn't belong to you.

As you continue to meditate, remember a time when you walked outside, hiked in the woods, or worked in the garden, you benefitted from a grounding happening all around you when you were present in nature. When not in the woods with all the trees, sounds and sights reminding you, you can use the image of a grounding cord to connect you to the Earth. Your grounding cord can be like sitting on a tree trunk. Let the roots of the tree be your grounding all the way to the center of the Earth. Imagine creating a connection between you and the Earth that not only brings you into your body to be present, it also creates a channel for you to effortlessly release anything you are ready to let go of by simply setting that intention. Let yourself be supported. The Universe has you!

Continue to release and relax, enjoying your grounding and connection to the Earth as you breathe and be. Let thoughts pop up as they do, see them, acknowledge them, and send them down your grounding cord as you feel ready. This is your meditation. No rules. Only what works and feels good to you.

When you are ready, create a protection bubble surrounding your body and some of the space around your body too. Let the bubble sit at the edge of your space, about two to three feet around your body. There is no right or wrong. Let yourself tune in to what feels right for you in this moment. Your grounding and protection bubble (or whatever image you use to represent a protection around your body and space) may change every time you meditate. That is okay. It is about paying attention to what pops up and giving yourself permission to see it. As you sit grounded and centered in your bubble, take a moment to observe what this feels like. Give yourself a few breaths here in this grounded, protected space.

As you continue in meditation, ask yourself: Do I feel safe? Do I feel centered? Do I feel at ease? How often do I give myself space?

Notice how having your own space changes things for you. Play with bringing your bubble closer and further away from your body. See how adjusting it feels to you. You can pop your bubble at any time and create a new one. Let the bubble be a filter for you to let in the energies you want and stop the energies you would rather not have in your space. You can change it up any time you want. This is your space.

Pause here to notice thoughts, feelings, and sensations in your body and take a few breaths as you continue to ground and sit in the center of your protection bubble.

As you meditate in this grounded and protected space you have created for yourself, see that you can call back your energy to fill your body and space. Visualize your energy pouring down into your body and space like the sun shining down its beautiful golden rays or rain sprinkling your energy on and around you. Whatever image works for you. Let your energy cascade all around you, filling and energizing your body and space with your energy, your unique vibration. If you see it as a color, lace it with gold. Let yourself shine! Notice how your body is feeling as your energy settles into your space. If your attention drifts and you find yourself thinking about something else, it is not a problem. Return your attention to your body, your grounding, your protection bubble and your energy filling your space, as you are ready. Notice what your energy feels like in your space. Let your thoughts go where they need to go, coming back to your breath, your grounding, your protection bubble, and your energy as you can. Tune in to the thoughts, pictures, feelings, and energies popping up. This is your meditation, yours to do and see whatever you wish.

As you ground and release energy, your gold sun energy fills you back in with your energy. Your energy is a healing to you. Grounding is a healing. Be in this meditative space for as long as it feels good to you. Know and trust that you can come back to this space anytime. You have now created a space for yourself to return to whenever the time is right.

Take a few deep breaths and as you are ready, open your eyes if they are closed and come out of meditation. Stretch, yawn, touch your toes, wiggle around a little, stand up, and move around as you come back to your body and this present time.

Meditation Tips and Tricks:

- There is never a wrong way or time to meditate (assuming you are in a safe place to do so, for example, not behind the wheel of a car).

- Start and end your day with grounding – the saying in my house goes "Let your grounding cord hit the floor before your feet."

- You may fall asleep at first while meditating and that is okay!

- Managing energy we encounter within and external to ourselves takes practice. It's okay if it doesn't feel natural or easy the first time. Keep going!

- The more you meditate, the gentler and faster you are able to know your information.

- As you practice these tools, the easier it becomes to recognize when you are not energetically tethered or grounded.

- As you connect to your energy, you will get quicker and quicker at noticing when you unintentionally allow energy that is not your own to invade your space as well as when you need a boost of your own energy during the day.

- Reminder, make meditation work for you! If it doesn't work for you, you won't practice. Take the techniques and make them your own.

- In meditation, time is not the same as on a linear body level. Some days a thirty-second meditation may be all you need, some days a three-hour meditation might not feel like enough. Focus less on length of time and more on how you feel and what you notice.

Questions after Meditating:

- What did you notice about your grounding cord and your energy?
- What images came up and stood out to you during the meditation?
- How does your body feel - before, during, and after meditating?
- What technique feels the best/resonates the most right now (keep in mind, over time this may change)?

Chapter 3: Body, Mind, and Spirit

Meditation offers an opportunity to go within, to get to know ourselves better and more fully. The techniques discussed thus far, when practiced, give tangible ways to tune in and develop a sense of knowing our own energy, our truth and our information. From the practice, we delve deeper into understanding and learning about and from our body, mind and spirit. We get to access the wealth of information there is to discover about ourselves, what guides us, what motivates us, what drives us, what inspires us and even what we are here to do, be, have and create.

Our body talks to us all the time. Most of the communication is on an unconscious level. We don't think about our heart beating, it does. We breathe automatically. We don't have to think about moving our foot out of the way when someone is about to accidentally step on our toes. All these things happen reflexively. There is no need to devote major amounts of thought or energy. And yet, when we consciously tune in to our bodies, we can get a lot of valuable information about our needs, our wants, what nurtures us, what energizes us, and what feels good to us.

Likewise, our minds, via our thoughts, are telling us things all the time. Rarely are we not seeing, noticing or gathering information in some fashion. Our mind processes things at different speeds – we see a red light and come to a stop quickly without even having to tell ourselves to stop. Other things might require more processing time. When your job asks you to take a position within the company located in another country, you might have to process and think about it. We call that analyzing. We get good at analyzing. As you get to know your mind, you decide when best to use your analyzing skills, and when to rely on your intuition to guide you.

When it comes to spirit, sometimes words do not exist to describe things. Our spirit represents our connection to our higher self, our higher sense of knowing. Our spirit communicates the energy of "I know, I'm not sure how, I just know." When you hear yourself saying this about knowing, your spirit is communicating with you. Spirit guides us whether we are aware of it or not. When it comes to spirit, our job is to listen and to receive the insights. The more you tune in to that aspect of who you are, the easier you may find it is to be on your path and to trust your intuition.

As I meditated more and more, I created ease with working in my body, mind, and spirit. I heard more clearly what my body, mind and spirit told me and I could more easily decipher, or read, my energy as opposed to other people's energy. By connecting with my body, mind, and spirit, my awareness of my intuition grew. With that growth, new discoveries and insights emerged with my next steps, my path, my purpose. When we connect to our inner voice, our unique energy we are able to listen to our inner wisdom, our higher self. The result is powerful, even life changing, and it all starts with connecting to body, mind, and spirit.

Connecting to Your Body

One of the most powerful side effects of practicing grounding and being present in meditation is the information we receive from our body. Our body is constantly communicating with us, telling us things that we sometimes miss. If we miss a message, the message might grow louder and louder until we have no other choice except to stop and listen. Have you ever felt like you needed to rest and didn't, and then you ended up getting injured in some way? When you ground regularly, you foster the creation of a space to listen to the communications from your body.

Running in general, and for certain a marathon, takes time. There are not too many ways around the preparation needed to complete one. You have to show up and train. While some may run faster than others, at the end of the day, the body requires the time commitment to prepare, train, recover, and repeat, mile after mile.

Training created time for me to connect to my body in a way I had not done before. As I ran mile after mile, as I stretched, grounded, hydrated, fueled up, and visualized, I noticed my body changing. As the training continued and we pushed into the high teens and low twenties on distances for weekend runs, I used the time to notice and observe my body. Although I had not completed a marathon before, my intuition told me I needed to pay attention to my body or risk not crossing the finish line. Training gave me time to ask myself: how are you feeling, what are you thinking about, and what are you noticing. As race day approached, caring for my body became a primary focus. I made sleep, overall health, and taking care of myself a top priority. I had trained 6 months for this day – I didn't want to jeopardize not running because of an injury or illness.

Our bodies are amazing. They are constantly doing things we don't always understand in the moment. They know more than we sometimes even realize. We don't always see or know what we are holding onto, preparing for or handling. Our bodies feed us information all the time and unless we give ourselves time and space to tune in and listen, we can miss the messages. The marathon reinforced what I learned in meditation: to pause, to be present, to honor what the body needs, to listen and to recognize shifting and changing.

Now, when my body craves something, I listen. When my body changes, I notice. I make a point to pay attention to what my body communicates to me. I don't always get the message, I ignore the communication at times, I still push it too far occasionally and I don't always accept the information it is telling me. I do my best each day to show up for my body, to listen, to respect, to honor and to care for it. Using a grounding cord is a big part of tuning in to my body, giving it a space to release and let go and ensuring that I am working with my energy. If we accept the idea that we all choose the body we have, then opportunity lies in listening and responding accordingly and to the best of our ability to what it is telling us and teaching us. Using meditation to reflect on communication from the body becomes invaluable along our path of developing and working with energy every day.

Connecting to Your Mind

We have many thoughts that pop up whether we want them to or not, when in meditation and not in meditation. We constantly perceive, notice, and take in information from our five senses (taste, touch, smell, sight, and sound). We often don't even realize the extent of what we filter through in a day.

My tagline is "real quick." It's a phrase I say often – sometimes I mean it, and sometimes it pops out of my mouth before I realize it because our minds work real quick. Before we know it, we can have a hundred thoughts about something that was introduced to us only moments ago. It's a blessing and a curse we must all work to navigate – the minefields of our minds!

Often I hear the response when talking about meditation, "I can't meditate because I have too much on my mind," or "I can't quiet the thoughts in my head." My response: "Don't!" We need our thoughts, our responses. They help us figure out our answers, our truths and the world around us. The goal is to foster thoughts that empower us on our path – to use our mind for our creations rather than spending time on what is not supporting us.

As we grow up, our thoughts shift as our perspective changes. We see things differently than when we were a child, a teenager, a young adult, a full grown adult, and beyond. We are inundated with information – our mind must sift through the influx to figure out what to keep close, what to file away, what to discard, what resonates with us and what doesn't. If we are lucky, we get chances to play and explore throughout our life: we taste different foods, travel to different places, and visit different people. Everything we experience helps us to decipher what matches us, what we want to take with us and what we want to leave behind.

Sometimes, we get caught up in other people's desires, interests or energy and take them on as our own. Remember that friend in high school who loved volleyball so much she convinced you to try out and you played even though you didn't love it? Or the family business that everyone works in that you don't have a knack for and yet you show up for every day? Or you find yourself parenting as your dad did, saying the same things to your children even though it doesn't feel right. Ideally, we realize sooner than later when something doesn't fit and we correct it to consciously align with what more authentically represents us in the present.

It can feel challenging to know what belongs to us, what we think versus what thoughts belong to others around us as we are bombarded with information on a daily basis. Our thoughts can get confused with what matches us versus others due to the high volume of ideas, marketing, and input coming at us. It takes practice deciphering what thoughts are ours and which ones belong to others. Sharing information and watching how others do things is helpful; however, at some point, we must figure out what we genuinely think, what we know and how we feel.

In meditation, you create a place to sift through the thoughts, feelings, and experiences, to discover your authentic responses and reactions, what you truly think and feel. The location to rest your attention when in mediation is the center of your head, home to neutrality or non-judgment. Neutrality, a key when sifting through thoughts, enables you to look at and explore thoughts, experiences, people and energies without judgment. When you observe from the center of your head, you instantly create distance, a buffer zone and a separation to respond versus react. Neutrality is the difference between responding versus reacting.

Imagine driving a car. You are in the driver seat pressed as close as possible to the dashboard. You are on high alert, arms tense, hands tightly gripping the steering wheel at ten and two. Now imagine pulling back a bit, relaxing your arms, making space between your torso and the steering wheel. Notice as you pull back that you can see more as your field of vision widens which gives you a longer response time. This exemplifies the concept of sitting in the center of your head. When your attention is resting at the front of your space, leaning over the steering wheel, you lose time and space to see fully and respond accordingly. When you sit and pull back, you give yourself space to see and perceive, which is what moving your attention to the center of your head offers. Sometimes the illusion of pressure to respond quickly, to act fast, can get to us. Using the center of your head, creating that sanctuary for neutrality and non-judgment, gives you a place to rejuvenate, to restore, to see, and decide how to respond.

Reacting is often the first response. Day to day incidents can demand immediate attention - the spilled drink, the argument over toys, the broken plate, the dropped cookie, the skinned knee, or at work, a client wants an answer right this minute or a meeting time abruptly changes. Each one of these moments represents an opportunity to respond versus react. Responding means taking a moment, pausing, pulling back (into the center of your head if not already there), taking a breath, and then navigating the situation. Seeing those moments from the center of your head offers the space to respond without judgment. Having neutrality helps to move through those life moments thoughtfully by responding versus reacting, a tangible difference that can be felt in the body and mind as less stress, less tension and more ease. With practice, we can sit and operate from this place regularly, daily or even all the time.

Every moment, we are given the option of how we perceive, think and respond to life. We get to decide how we view and feel about things. Using the center of your head, shifting your perspective and noticing your thoughts are all ways to connect to your mind. The more you practice working from this space, the more easily you know your thoughts and find clarity in knowing your truths and your answers versus other people's truths and answers.

When we are children, we usually know ourselves well. We don't get easily influenced about when to start walking as an infant based on when our friend starts walking. We go at our own pace as a toddler. We try to do things the way we want, we dress how we want to look and so on. Somewhere between toddlerhood and adolescence, this evolves. We start noticing what others think or feel about us which can precipitate how we begin to think or feel about ourselves. At some point, ideally, we graduate out of concerning ourselves too much with what others think and instead bring the focus back to what we ourselves think and feel about something. That doesn't mean the constant bombardment of information present in day-to-day life doesn't penetrate our psyche in some way or another. Staying true to our thoughts, our feelings and our beliefs takes intention and attention.

In high school, I wanted to go to a certain college because I thought my Grandfather would have wanted me to go there. I applied to the school, interviewed and felt confident about everything. When the letter arrived saying I had not gotten in, I didn't know what to do. I thought I was supposed to go to that school. I didn't realize I was making a decision based on what I thought someone else wanted me to do. It wasn't my truth. At eighteen, I couldn't see that. I hadn't practiced knowing if something was a decision I was making because it lined up with what I wanted, needed or thought versus what others wanted, needed or thought.

I had practiced unconsciously tuning in to what others wanted, needed or thought without realizing it. The lesson around this experience I embarked on related to letting go of what we think we are supposed to do. When I released what I thought I was supposed to do, options opened up and I ended up at the right institution for me. I could have forced the other decision by waiting, applying again, even transferring; basically putting lots of effort into something that ultimately wasn't the right fit for me. I was able to avoid spending lots of time trying to find a way into the school when I opted for the path of least resistance and accepted admission to another school.

Our minds are powerful. We create millions of thoughts and ideas a day. We have so many, it is sometimes challenging to track where they all come from - and sometimes the origins are not important. Sometimes we lock into an idea, a thought, and we don't shift even when signs, people, even ourselves, are telling us we need to course correct. When I realigned myself with the college I eventually attended, I realized I had unconsciously responded to the flow of energy guiding me in a different direction. Through meditation, I have recognized the paths that are meant for us are often lined with ease and less effort. When we move in chorus with the energy around us, we take advantage of that ease.

When I refer to effort, I don't mean to imply that you don't need to work, that everything comes to you when you sit back and do nothing, that to pass the test, you don't need to study, or to receive the promotion, you can show up late every day. You have to show up in life. Showing up for the things that we want to do, the ideas we want to create, the path that is in our best interest, is a different sort of effort than trying to make things work, effort. When we try, I see an image of someone putting a round peg in a square hole. You can try all day to fit the wrong shape into the hole and while ultimately you might make it happen, what have you gained? When effort creeps into my space, it serves as a reminder to take note of what I am doing and lends itself to a minor or major course correction. When I operate in my body and space with my thoughts and feelings, I know more consciously the direction I wish to go. I move on the path with less effort than when I try to force a path that isn't mine. When things shift to feeling hard, cumbersome, clumsy or full of angst and frustration, it serves as a red flag, a warning, a reminder to pause, notice, pay attention and adjust. If your thoughts are yours, you can change them. If you can't change the thoughts, they are not yours. You can shift your energy and your experience of things. You cannot shift what is not yours to shift.

When I didn't get into the college I thought was my first choice, I relatively easily shifted to an alternative path. Now I realize I followed the energy of the situation. I went where things were moving, where there was momentum and ease. Life moves in a rhythm. When we can tune into that rhythm we remove stress, strain and effort. When we align our mindset with what is unfolding, we create space to navigate life with more ease and grace, and less effort. Our thoughts are powerful. When we notice them, connect with them, listen to them, and understand what our mind is saying to us, we gain insight and understanding into our path.

All this doesn't mean that everything is automatically easy from here forward if you simply align with your thoughts and incorporate neutrality into your life. It does mean you get to notice when effort creeps into your space, and follow where the energy is flowing to avoid it. When you consciously notice what thoughts keep coming back to you, where your attention returns, you start to see patterns and get a better understanding of what you are doing and creating. If you feel lost or stuck, not living the life you wanted, you have disconnected from your thoughts, your passions or your ideas. The parts of life that don't resonate represent openings to gather insight, information and awareness about who you are, what you love, what lifts you up, and what helps you take next steps on your journey. Taking stock of all that avails itself to us, seeing opportunities and reasons for different things happening along the way represent sources of learning and growing. If we take a no mistakes mindset approach, we see everything as a chance to know more. How we think and see things becomes paramount. Our thoughts determine how we view the life that unfolds. When we consciously make connections, we influence how we move through our life. As things unfold, we practice deciding how we view things. When we do this, our experience of what follows shifts. In choosing how we see things, changing our perspective and our thoughts, we alter how we experience what follows.

One of the ways to foster shifting our mindset is by bringing the energy of curiosity into our lives. Curiosity is a neutral energy. When you come from a pure place of curiosity, you are neutral. Think Curious George, that adorable monkey who was always so curious. He was not judgmental in the least. He simply possessed an enormous amount of curiosity about the world - he wanted to see and know everything! When curiosity is your guide, not only do you find neutrality, you discover and see differently. When wanting to see the world from fresh eyes like children have, bring curiosity into your life.

I got to practice this skill of seeing everything as an opportunity to grow and know more while on the way to my brother's wedding weekend. My family's minivan ended up going off the road and hitting a tree. At the time, my husband was driving and I was in the back middle row sitting next to our 4-month old son in his car seat while our three daughters ranging in age from two to six years old sat in the third row. Three times during the week leading up to the wedding, I had the intention of getting my brother and his soon to be wife a bag of their favorite red gummy candy. Three times that week, I had walked out of a store without the bag at which point I decided to forget about the candy. We woke up that Friday morning, loaded up the car, and started our three-hour drive up to Vermont. After several rest stops, we were almost there. Climbing the last incline, I had an overwhelming feeling that we were not going to get there. I am not one who panics, yet in this moment, my heart started to race and I felt anxious.

I decided to meditate. I closed my eyes and grounded, took a few deep breaths, and attempted to look at what I was feeling. Next thing I knew, we were heading toward a tree off the road and into a ditch. Although my husband managed to steer the car to avoid us hitting a tree head on, the impact caused airbags to deploy, leaving us mostly uninjured and stunned. As we exited the car with a little help from other motorists who stopped when they saw what happened, we collected ourselves on the side of the road and another car pulled over to help. As the driver and her college-aged daughter approached us, the daughter immediately got an idea and said, "Stay there, I know what you need. Stay right there!" She proceeded to go back to her car to grab something. She returned holding out a bag insisting, "You need this. Trust me, this is what you need." As I looked at what she handed me, I saw it was a bag of the exact red gummy candy I had intended to pick up for my brother all week. I could not believe what had happened. On the side of a road on a mountain in Vermont, a stranger had handed me a bag of the candy I had intended to purchase the days leading up to the trip.

Everything eased in that instant. I had an overwhelming sense of knowing that everything would be okay. We were where we were supposed to be and I needed to trust the process. The power of that experience shifted all that followed. While accidents are never fun, no one was seriously injured, we would make it to the weekend of wedding events and figure out logistics. In that moment, we replaced victim and fear thinking with thoughts of abundance and love. In shifting our perspective, we altered how we experienced all the challenges that followed too - getting six people to the wedding with no car in the middle of Vermont, for starters. Instead of being upset, anxious and angry, we felt gratitude and appreciation. We focused on what was right in our day. We were safe. It was a beautiful, sunny day and we would make it to the wedding.

The power of the mind is endless. When an event occurs, how we view it, experience it, and open ourselves up to responding to it changes what unfolds. The center of the head and working with curiosity represent two techniques to aid in our challenge of responding versus reacting and seeing opportunity. Harnessing and directing our thoughts toward the images, pictures, and energies we want to have, create, and experience in our lives leads to powerful manifesting. If you can see it, image it, create it - you can have it. It starts with a thought, a picture, from the mind. When you adjust your thinking, the experience that follows adjusts in response. Using meditation to tune in to your mind benefits every aspect of your life on your path toward working with energy every day.

Connecting to Your Spirit

When we turn our attention to spirit, things become less tangible. The body and mind are easier to understand - the body can be seen and we are familiar with our thought patterns and philosophies. Spirit is nonphysical. We cannot touch it and are rarely trained to recognize when our spirit, or our soul, is speaking to us. Spirit is also a term used to talk about ghosts and energies that have passed yet may still linger in the physical world. For our purposes, spirit will refer to the nonphysical part of ourselves connected to our physical body and mind, also known as our higher power, our higher level of consciousness or awareness. Our spirit guides us, directs us on our path, and facilitates our connection with our soul's purpose. When we have an awareness of what our spirit is communicating with us, we more fully experience the life we are here to create and fosters body-mind-spirit integration.

Time is a construct we experience on a body and mind level. In spirit, there is no time and space. When we sleep, we experience a bit of that essence. Have you ever woken up thinking twenty minutes have passed only to find out three hours had gone by? That is how spirit operates – no time and space. In spirit, possibilities are endless, every idea has merit and we can do it all. This is vital to our wellbeing! We need hope; we need spirit buoying us. There is no accident that the common phrase is "keep your spirits up" as those spirits help us to navigate life and forge ahead.

Sometimes there is no way to adequately describe spirit. In spirit, we walk through walls, we climb Mt. Everest without training and we fly. It's on the physical and mental levels (in the body and in the mind) that we are limited by time and space, to physical constructs such as walls, relying on airplanes or are bound by our Earthly knowledge of what is possible. Spirit knows no bounds making it tough to tie down to our two-dimensional vocabulary.

One word that often works in Spirit is "yes." Saying yes raises the energetic vibration, and whenever you do that, you create openness, willingness and movement. When working in spirit, limits disappear and the possibilities are endless. "Yes" is a way to bring about change and create momentum. In other words, it brings spirit to the physical planes of the body and mind to essentially open up possibilities.

After yes, the next step is making room for what you want to manifest. If you want a puppy, you start going to dog kennels, talking to friends or dog breeders; you bring the energy of a dog into your life through your actions, your words and your intent. In effect, you create space. If there is no room for something, it won't come into being. In Feng Shui, the study of bringing harmony into your environment, if you want to develop a romantic relationship, it is suggested to have a nightstand on both sides of your bed to foster a place for a partner. When you make room for someone or something in your life in advance, it makes it easier for that person or thing to come into being.

Meditation is a place to say "yes" and receive messages spirit wants to share. It is the training ground for bringing messages from spirit to consciousness. Meditation is a way to listen and to receive, in order to then manifest on body and mind levels. The way, the manner, the style, the time or the place you meditate doesn't matter as long as it works for you. As you practice saying yes and visualizing what you want to create in meditation, a key energy that works well in the body, mind, and spirit is amusement. Amusement is light-heartedness, not taking things too seriously (and in this regard, amusement helps in a lot of situations beyond meditation). Amusement does not mean that everything is funny, rather it means connecting to that place inside each of us where we can have levity and ease.

Tapping into the energy of amusement promotes spirit connection. Spirit is light, airy, open. Amusement mirrors the energy of spirit. Bringing that energy into a meditation practice, into life, keeps things from getting stuck, from feeling overwhelming and fosters the flow of insights. The purpose of amusement is not to laugh at everything. It is to have a way to navigate life with greater ease. It reminds us to not take everything too seriously. Bringing in the energy of yes into your life, visualizing yourself manifesting, creating and doing, all from a place of lightness and joyful curiosity, leads to promoting movement and flow.

Like everything, amusement is energy too. If we connect to the energy or vibration of amusement, we shift the energy and experience of stressful moments, intense times and challenges that arise. When things are lighter, they are easier to process, to digest, to see and to move through. This isn't to say that heartbreaking events are all of a sudden made light, that tragedy and hardships are a joke, that feeling deep sadness is wrong or unhealthy. It can be quite the opposite. Rather amusement helps lighten the burden of the situation at hand if you are seeking that relief. If you can call on and connect to the energy of amusement, especially when things feel challenging or stuck, you have another coping strategy, another tool in your toolbox.

I have a tendency toward being serious. I love to laugh and joke; however, I have a serious side to me. At times, that side takes over. When I am able to notice this and bring in amusement, it instantly makes things feel less intense. Sometimes, I forget, as, like most things in life, it takes practice.

I am the middle child of two brothers. One night, my older brother came home with a couple of friends after swim practice. My parents happened to be out and my younger brother and I didn't think this was such a good idea. We were all in high school – my older brother and I seniors and my younger brother a freshman – of the age that we could be trusted to be home alone. And yet, here was my brother bringing friends home on a school night after swim practice when my parents were not home. My younger brother and I couldn't believe he was flouting the rules. Rather than immediately calling to report him to our parents, we decided to be productive and make our lunches for the next school day in hopes that as we wrapped that up, our older brother would see the error of his ways and his friends would head home.

As we made sandwiches, we discussed the situation and found our amusement, which in this situation came in the form of putting candy in our older brother's sandwich. The next day at school he would get a weird tasting surprise that we thought was a riot. We laughed as we prepared his sandwich and packed it up. As the mood lightened, the friends went home and we carried on with the night. The next day, he enjoyed his bespoke sandwich and to this day we laugh about the silliness of it all. At the time, I didn't realize we were using the power of amusement to shift the energy of the situation. We found lightness, in the midst of something that felt challenging and uncomfortable.

While that is a trivial example, it became a tangible one for me. In more serious life events, finding amusement might feel more difficult. Start small. Let yourself notice when lightening up a situation is possible and welcomed, and go from there.

Amusement does not negate the power of experiencing or feeling other energies and emotions like anger, fear, and frustration. They all have a place as do love, excitement, and happiness. Tuning in to the energies we experience empowers us to decide which energies we pay attention to or feed. By adding amusement to our repertoire of energies, we invite spirit into our space. When we welcome yeses, let ourselves imagine and visualize, have light heartedness and amusement, we welcome spirit and enlightenment in the process. Spirit is always there. It's up to us to receive it and listen. It doesn't have to take hours; it doesn't have to be hard. Working with energy every day can be light, fun, instantaneous and, yes, amusing.

Meditation: Body, Mind, Spirit

In this mediation, let's look at neutrality, curiosity and amusement as techniques to foster integration of body, mind and spirit. Neutrality is one of the best energies to work with in meditation and in life. When you have neutrality about something, you create space for non-judgment thus welcoming in curiosity. The energy of amusement lightens the mood and keeps things moving. Let's get started working with these techniques as they work in chorus to deliver messages to inspire you along your path toward mindfulness, awareness and purpose.

Settle into your body, taking a deep breath or two, closing your eyes, however that feels comfortable to you. As you lengthen your breath, imagine a grounding cord connecting you to the center of the Earth, instantly and effortlessly. Visualize the grounding cord in any form you choose supporting your body, creating a path to release and let go of anything you might be ready to part with at this time.

When you are ready, rest your attention on an object in your vicinity. You can have your eyes opened or closed as you notice that object. Rest your attention on the object. Then move your attention to your body. Resting your attention on your body, take a breath or two. Then move your attention to your nose. Pausing for a breath as you rest your attention on your nose. Next, move your attention to the bridge of your nose, the spot between your eyes, and from that point, draw your attention straight back to rest your attention directly in the center of your head. This is a place for neutrality, non-judgment. This is a space for you, a sanctuary for you to rest, to notice, to see from neutrality and non-judgment. Create this space for you - envision what it looks like - decorate it, own it, make it comfy and cozy for you! As you settle into this space, notice what it feels like to be in the center of your head, to have your attention resting behind your eyes. You can sit in this space when in and even when not in meditation. This is a space you can re-side in whenever and however long you like. You can operate from the center of your head all day long. Working from this space creates an opportunity for responding versus reacting, for seeing without judging, for noticing versus deciding. The center of your head is a space for you, no one else needs to enter. This is yours. Pop into the center of your head in meditation when looking to gather insight about a situation and throughout the day. Play with it and make it work for you.

As you sit grounded and in the center of your head, notice how your body feels, what thoughts pop up and what messages enter your con-sciousness. There is no right or wrong here. If you drift out, you can re-turn without any effort. Simply bring your attention back to the bridge of your nose and draw it straight back into the center of your head. This is your space, for you and you alone. As you make it yours, notice it will be easier and easier to jump into your center of head. You will be able to move in and out as you wish throughout your day. Using this space to connect and see, to intuit and listen, to release and energize.

As you relax into this meditation, notice thoughts or feelings pop-ping up and allow yourself to be curious. Explore what is coming to your consciousness. Ask questions. Observe. Notice. This is your time to connect with the thoughts, images and pictures showing up for you. Ap-proach the information with curiosity to discover and gain insight.

As you are in the center of your head, allow yourself to bring in amusement. Let yourself picture it by asking yourself what amusement looks like. It could be a color, a symbol, a texture, a shape, a sound or any image that pops in your head in or out of meditation. Once you have that picture, you can bring it to your awareness whenever you need amusement to lighten things up. You can imagine it sprinkling into your space as the color or symbol, swirling around your space like ribbons or filling your space like you are swimming in a pool of amuse-ment.

As you let amusement fill your space, see a moment from your mind's eye of a time you said "yes," when you were presented with an opportunity and you enthusiastically went with it. How did it feel? What does the energy of the word "yes" feel like in your space? How does "yes" feel in your body? What thoughts pop up? What messages surface?

On the flip side, recount a time when you were told "no" or you said "no" to an opportunity. What did or does that look like? How does your body feel? What thoughts pop in when you see that experience? No is an energy just like yes. They both have a time and place. Notice what the energy of no feels and looks like in your body and space.

Each time you see a picture from your mind's eye, you can ask questions to develop it further and follow it. When you have gotten all you need from the picture, you can release it down your grounding cord or envision it dissolving in front of you. The pictures you see in meditation represent an avenue for insight and enlightenment. Let the pictures and your curiosity guide your meditation.

Next, ask yourself what you would like to manifest or create in your life? In meditation, sitting in the center of your head, looking out from your mind's eye from neutrality and non-judgment let a picture or pictures form. See what unfolds when you ask yourself what you want to manifest and create. It may be something you knew or something brand new.

As thoughts surface in your meditation, bring your attention back to the center of your head anytime your mind drifts away. There is no time and space in meditation. Let yourself be present, flowing with your meditation, receiving insights, thoughts, pictures, and information as they come.

This is a space you can return to anytime. You can ground, be in the center of your head, welcoming amusement and lightheartedness into your space, while seeing and creating pictures of all you want to manifest. When you can see it, you can create it and have it. It starts with a vision, a picture. You can create that picture right here, in meditation, from your mind's eye, from a grounded, centered space, full of the energies you would like to see in your today and tomorrow. You have created a place to practice, to visualize, to see and to manifest. Let yourself have this space anytime, anywhere and every day.

Take a few more deep breaths, letting yourself soak up this space you have created for yourself and when you are ready, open your eyes. While coming out of meditation, yawn and stretch as you connect back with your body and your surroundings.

Meditation Tips and Tricks:

- When it comes to meditation and spirit, there are no rules.

- Meditation can be done in the morning, in the night, during the day, after a cup of coffee, before a cup of coffee, when you can't sleep, when you only want to sleep, when you are upset, happy, sad, afraid or excited.

- Meditation can be done sitting, standing, lying down, on a train or on a plane.

- There are so many styles and ways to meditate, the most important being that it resonates and works for you.

- As you practice working in the center of your head and bringing amusement into your space, saying yes and visualizing what you want to manifest, things will shift and change.

- Some shifts may be subtle; others may be more obvious. Tune in to your body, mind and spirit even out of meditation to receive messages and insights.

Questions after Meditating:

- What did you notice about your grounding cord this time around?

- How did it feel to be in the center of your head? Did you notice a shift in your perspective when sitting in the center of your head?

- How might you use the center of your head and amusement every day?

- Do you say "yes" often? Is that an energy you like to work with regularly?

- Do you notice yourself saying "no" frequently? What did looking at no in meditation bring up for you?

4

Chapter 4: Intuition

Now that we have practiced working with energy through honing meditation techniques such as grounding, using our own vibrational energy and have explored the trinity of the body, mind and spirit connection, let's now focus on intuition. Understanding our intuition will prepare us for our next adventure - reading energy.

Looking at energy intuitively is how we begin to read it and gain insights. Three main ways we experience our intuition are via empathic abilities (feeling energy), clairaudience (hearing energy) and clairvoyance (seeing energy). We all intuit in different ways. We may have preferences for one way that comes more naturally to us, but rest assured we can all employ each of the three abilities, especially if we intentionally work toward developing them in meditation.

Feeling to Know: Empathic Intuition

When we relate to the emotions of others deeply almost as if they are our own, this is empathy. We all have it to some degree and can develop it as much as we like. Those of us who primarily bring in information this way are known as empaths. When you are an empath, you may find you pick up on people's feelings and energies without always knowing it. You walk into a room and immediately have a headache only to discover that the person standing across the room has had a headache all morning. When out running errands in a busy town center, you suddenly feel upset with no clue as to why or where the feeling came from only to turn the corner to see a child lost and sobbing. You recognize a friend feeling sad before she may have even processed her emotions over not being picked for that promotion. When you connect with her on this, she asks how you knew.

Empathic abilities are powerful and profound. When conscious of them, they empower us. When we are not aware or in control of them, they can have debilitating effects ranging from feeling emotionally overwhelmed to downright scared. You may worry you are not in charge of how you feel, making you wary of meeting new people and increasing your desire to avoid crowded places.

As a child, I remember picking up on other people's energy, which translated into stomachaches in my body. I did not have words to describe how I sponged up these feelings, yet I knew it made me uncomfortable emotionally and physically. Although I would not label myself as shy, I loved staying at home. Typical childhood favorites such as sleepovers and field trips unnerved me. The more I learned about energy, the more I understood why soaking up the energies of others as an adolescent felt so taxing and why it always amplified when I was away from home surrounded by unfamiliar people.

Energy is everywhere always. In our personal spaces and daily lives, we are saturated with the energies of others. We are bombarded and asked to pay attention to energies in spaces not previously accessed. We sit in our homes scrolling the Internet, checking work emails, posting on social media, and absorbing television all hours of the day. We have allowed our modern, tech-forward society to enter and invade our private spaces without limit. Neighbors used to visit and chat over fences to share life updates. Now you hear about their tropical vacation and homegrown veggies from their social media pages. News primarily came in the form of newspapers and the network evening news a couple decades ago, arriving at only a few possible and precise times of the day when your newspaper was delivered or when the news was broadcast. News now breaks every minute, runs 24/7, and is pushed as alerts to our smartphones no matter the time.

Our communication and interactions have drastically shifted over the last few decades, which on an energy level has changed the landscape of our downtime and our ability to unplug from the energies of our day, especially as empaths. I remember in college being able to disconnect for a weekend, unplug, and go off the grid by shutting down my desktop. This gave me the space and time to rest and reconnect with my own energy. I could relax and have "me" time. With all this connectivity, we need to get smarter about giving ourselves time to disconnect, get better at noticing energy's impact on us, and get more determined to stay true to our own unique energy vibration. Meditating recharges our energy as we use techniques to center ourselves to return to our empathic, intuitive selves, regardless of the barrage of outside energy.

Hearing to Know: Clairaudience

Clairaudience is the ability to hear things not said out loud. You hear a phone ring in your head and then the actual phone rings. You can't get that random song out of your head and going to lunch hear it in the elevator for the first time in years. You have a thought emerge on an obscure subject you have no reason to ponder, except when you say it out loud a person you are with says he was thinking the same thing. When these clairaudience experiences happen to individuals, it is easy to chalk them up to coincidences. While some may be that, some are very likely our intuition talking to us, even prompting us to tune in and hone our energetic listening skills.

Have you ever felt like everywhere you went, you heard the same message? Perhaps not always directed at you, yet the same or similar words found their way to your ears? Tuning in to messages you are hearing around you that mean something or carry a message for you is also clairaudience.

The power of tapping into our own clairaudience is in hearing our own answers. Our information can signal to us we are on the "right" path. It is great to intuit that the phone is going to ring. However, it has potentially more impact to hear your inner voice providing guidance on which job offer to accept or which university to attend. Practicing keying in to energy and listening in meditation is the best way to continue to develop your intuition with the help of clairaudience.

Seeing to Know: Clairvoyance

Clairvoyance is the ability to see energy clearly. It is the ability to conjure pictures relating to specific energies in your mind's eye. An example of clairvoyance is when someone tells you a story and you picture aspects of it. Our clairvoyance activates when we see ourselves living in a new house with no conscious plans for moving. Three months later, we are transferred to a new city by our employer and settle into a new home. Another example is we may randomly think of an iguana and later on, while watching TV, a character on a show has a pet iguana. Stranger still, the next morning out of the blue, you see an old friend, Ross, a few customers ahead of you at the coffee shop and he has an iguana on his t-shirt. You decide to initiate a conversation even if you are a few minutes late to your next meeting. Staying and catching up just feels right. You and Ross easily pick up where you left off years ago. It feels like kismet.

If you are flexing your clairvoyance, you may too see symbols connected to certain words or phrases, and you may see colors, known as auras, surrounding people. Some clairvoyants see colors all the time, others have worked on being able to turn their gifts on or off by choice.

Clairvoyance is associated with being psychic and being able to predict the future. At the core, it is about seeing energy in present time, seeing what is unfolding now which can inform the future.

As an energy reader and healer, I believe in free will and that the power of reading and seeing energy is not in predicting the future, rather in seeing energy and looking at next steps. When you see the energy, you know how to move forward. If you see the energy behind something, you better understand how to navigate through it.

Before I knew to identify myself as a clairvoyant, I saw and knew things. I visited Chicago for a business trip and as I ran by the lake, I saw myself living there. Sure enough, six months later, I moved. A picture appeared, as I ran, of me living there and I knew it would happen. I didn't know how or when. The picture represented my first mindful step on my clairvoyant journey where I saw a picture and knew the next step that would line up when the time was right.

Developing Your Abilities

There isn't one right way to work with intuitive abilities. The opportunity is in opening up to your abilities, which we all have, and working with them in your meditation practice every day. Being an empath doesn't mean you have to walk around feeling everyone's feelings 24/7; being clairaudient doesn't mean you must hear people's thoughts without end; being clairvoyant doesn't mean you see everyone's pictures in a constant slideshow. They can be practiced, honed and used to assist you in your life, with your goals and your endeavors. If you decide to branch out into energy work and healing, you can assist others in receiving guidance on their life path as you develop too.

One reason we might disconnect from our innate intuitive abilities is that we get overwhelmed. Remember sitting in high school math class and completely zoning out? You wanted to follow along, you attempted to stay focused, you did your best and yet there was too much information coming at you. Before you knew it, you had checked out. When we are younger, we are much more in tune with our energy and our feelings. We know when we are hungry, we cry when we feel sad, we laugh when we want. As we get older, the inundation of news and information referenced earlier mixed with our adult responsibilities makes for busy, hectic days. We seldom pause to purge what we no longer need to only carry the essentials with us. We tend to carry all this weight all day long, maybe taking a break at the end of the day by going for a walk, talking with a friend or laughing at the dinner table. If we don't take a break or release what no longer serves us, we work through it all night and carry it into the next day. We remain overloaded.

Meditation techniques, such as a grounding cord, serve as a way to release and let information we don't need go as we learned earlier. Another way to clear out energy is through creating and destroying. We are constantly creating and destroying, whether we realize it or not. Using the concept of creating and destroying as a way of clearing and releasing energy keeps us and our energies moving.

We wake up and create our day and go to bed after destroying the day when it is over and done. Without creation, there isn't destruction and vice versa. Creating and destroying, when used in meditation, serve as a yin and yang technique to release energy, get unstuck and clear out energetic "gunk" that gets caught up in your space. If we are energetically holding too much in our space, we can't bring in the new. Physically, if we have our hands full, we can't pick something else up. When it comes to energy, it isn't always as obvious when we are energetically overstuffed in our bodies and minds. We can carry this unconsciously. When we are energetically full, we seem distracted, detached, overwhelmed, flustered, tired, annoyed, frantic, depressed and anxious.

Through this meditation technique of creating and destroying, we energetically disconnect from different energies in order for them to come back together in a form we can see, understand, process or release. When we look at a picture, we transform the energy into a shape, symbol or feeling to see and better understand.

Children create and destroy all the time. A two year old builds a tower and then knocks it down, laughing all the while. To her, it is hysterical. Create it and destroy it. Repeat over and over for endless fun. Fast forward two or three years, that same child now wants the tower to stay up and when a little sibling comes over and accidentally knocks over the tower, tears and tantrum erupt. She got attached to her creation and forgot about the power of creating and destroying as a natural and empowering cycle. Using the technique of creating and destroying in meditation reminds us of the power of that cycle, of how helpful creating and destroying is to our forward progress and growth as well as to staying unstuck and present in our lives.

Meditation: Creating and Destroying

In this mediation, let's look at the power of creating and destroying as a way to clear energy from our space that doesn't belong to us and create room for more of our own energy or energy we deliberately invite into our space. Using this technique allows us to further hone our intuition to better detect and receive incoming information.

As you settle into your space, closing your eyes and taking a deep breath or two, notice your grounding cord and see that you can create an image of a sun above your head that fills you in with your energy or imagine your unique color vibration raining down upon you. See your unique energy vibration flowing down into your body and space. Let yourself receive your energy into your space, seeing and trusting that your energy knows exactly where to go and what to do. You can be present, grounded and receiving your energy as a healing to you. Your energy rejuvenates and restores you as it settles back into your space. You can be sitting in the center of your head, seeing your energy filling your body and the space surrounding you. Notice how your body feels, where your mind goes and what your spirit says as you let your meditation practice unfold.

From your mind's eye, create a visual or an image of an object, a bubble or a symbol or shape that appears out in front of you - it can be any image, color, size, shape. Once you see it, notice that you can destroy it, without any effort, simply blow it up, evaporate it, dissolve it or eliminate it however you choose. Then, see you can create another object, bubble or symbol, maybe the same color, maybe different. There is no right or wrong, simply create it, see it and then destroy it. Just like that, knowing energy is neither created nor destroyed. This concept gives you space to restructure and reshape energy, to see things differently, to recreate what was in order to have the new that is coming in.

If we never let go of the day, we would never have tomorrow and so on. We would be constantly stuck in today. Creating and destroying shifts the energy of a stressful situation, energizes you if you are feeling tired and aids in releasing tension and stress. Notice as you create and destroy what shifts in your body, mind and spirit. Tune in to what feelings are popping up, what pictures are appearing in front of your mind's eye and what messages you are intuiting. Your body might feel lighter, your shoulders may relax or you may unconsciously even twitch.

As you create and destroy, you may not know all the places you are clearing out stuck or stagnant energy from your body and space. You can ask what you are clearing, what energy is moving out of your space,

and see pictures that pop up as you ask yourself questions. Let your cu-
riosity guide you.

If you feel particularly stuck in a certain energy, you can imagine
that specific energy out in front of you, in a bubble or as an object of
your choice and then destroy it. For example, put frustration or anger
in your creation. See it, maybe it is a different color than the other ob-
jects you have created, no judgment – no right or wrong – your atten-
tion resting in the center of your head, seeing whatever pops up as you
set the intention for this object to represent frustration or anger. When
you are ready, destroy it. See it evaporating, exploding, even dissolving
into mist right in front of your eyes. Feel the energy release from your
space. You might notice right away a part of your body relaxes. Take a
deep breath and see if anything else feels different. You are releasing
energy through this visual technique of creating and destroying.

Take a few deep breaths, noticing how your body and space have
shifted. What feels different? What feels the same? Is there a color or
a picture that pops up revealing insight or information to you about a
question that you have wondered?

Stay in this space as long as it feels good to you. Create objects, pic-
tures, images, symbols, shapes and then destroy them. Get comfortable
with creating and destroying. When you are ready to come out of med-
itation, open your eyes, yawning and stretching. Stand up and come
back to your body.

Meditation Tips and Tricks:

- You can create and destroy in meditation while walking, while
working, at the end of the day, at the beginning of the day and all
throughout the day.
- Creating and destroying is a technique to move and clear energy.
- The more you play with this technique, the more it can work
for you.

- Employ this technique as you transition from activity to activity during your day to mark the beginning and end to events - see one event dissolve in front of you before you go to the next.

- Let creating and destroying foster clarity and focus as you release through blowing up, dissolving or evaporating energies that don't belong in your space.

Questions after Meditating:

- What did it feel like to create?
- What did it feel like to destroy?
- Is one easier than the other?
- How did your body respond to the visual of creating and destroying?
- When your thoughts drift, is creating and destroying helpful to reset and re-center?
- How can you use the concept of creating and destroying to assist you in your life to facilitate smoother transitions and next steps?

5

Chapter 5: Permission

Permission is an amazing energy worth exploring before moving on to reading energy intuitively in meditation. When we give ourselves permission, or the opening, to do something, to have something, to create something, it is magical, transformative and validating. It also creates a smoother and more direct path to having what you desire.

One of the things about energy is that we all work with it, consciously or unconsciously. Along my path as an energy reader and healer, I also learned the skill of mediumship, or communication with the non-physical spirits of those who have passed on. Or, yes, ghosts. I have often had people comment that they couldn't see what I see or connect to spirits like I do. What strikes me when I hear this is that only the notion of permission separates us. Where does permission come from and how do we expand it for ourselves so we can connect to our energy and our information in meditation?

Growing up, we all have different levels of permission. Perhaps your friend had permission to bike across town when they were 10 while you had to wait until you were 13. That type of permission was probably spelled out as rules. The type of permission I reference is more subtle. It might have been conveyed through indirect comments such as "you could do that, however...," or "I wouldn't do that if I were you." Comments or suggestions made by people in our lives that hint to their feelings often passively might inadvertently limit our permission to undertake a challenge, express ourselves and just be who we want to be. Somewhere along the way, we internalize external messages telling us that what we want to do, create or have is wrong. So we deny ourselves that permission without reflecting on its origin.

When we get shut down (ever have a really great idea and you rush off to tell someone and they mock or discredit it?), it hurts. After a few times of getting shut down, we may stop advancing in that direction due to the rejection or we may quit altogether shutting off (consciously or unconsciously) a part of ourselves.

The repetitive denial of permission can lead to tendencies or patterns later in life that need healing. We heal by giving ourselves permission once again. When was the last time you gave yourself permission to be silly, to laugh out loud all day long, to sleep until noon, to stay up late or to have a second piece of cake? It matters less the activity, as it is more about welcoming the energy of permission into your life.

Once permission is granted, that which was elusive or taboo might not be such a scary big deal after all. The cookie you resisted, once you have permission to eat, may. not seem that appealing. If only we had given ourselves permission sooner instead of expending time and energy on avoidance or denial.

Clearing Resistance

When we give ourselves permission, things are easier. Permission destroys resistance. When we don't want to do something or feel we have to do something, we unconsciously create resistance. Notice resistance when you feel your body tighten up or you find yourself clenching your jaw at the thought or mention of something unpleasant. Resistance alerts you to look deeper, to explore and ask questions. Sometimes we resist something that might turn out to be in our best interest. Learning to recognize what resistance feels like and looks like in your body and space gives you the chance to move past it to find what lies beyond. Then you can destroy it if you choose.

I resisted getting a dog. We had a full household and enjoyed the ability to jump in the car and head out at the spur of the moment. When my children started asking more regularly and making reasonable arguments as to why we should add a dog to our family, I made a beeline to my meditation chair. I had to look at and make sense of my resistance. I am all for manifesting and creating, so why not let the children manifest a dog?

Sometimes we double down on resisting. We resist uncovering what we are actively resisting. In this case, thankfully, I persisted in getting more clarity. As I settled into my grounding cord and rested my attention behind my eyes in the center of my head, I asked for pictures to illuminate my resistance surrounding a dog. I let myself see the energy that was present in my space and pictures began to emerge. As soon as I let the images roll through my mind's eye, I could see what was holding me back.

Resistance had created the illusion of a wall. I couldn't go further until I looked at it more closely. When I did, I saw a picture of fear that I might fail. I didn't grow up with dogs, what if I couldn't handle it? Once I saw and acknowledged the fear picture, it evaporated. I could then see beyond my resistance to the growth that could result for our family as a whole and individually. I saw a picture of my son doing his homework with our dog resting beside him in the years to come. I saw my youngest daughter running and laughing with the dog in the backyard. I saw my eldest saying goodbye to the dog as she headed off to college and me finding comfort in our dog's presence. All these pictures flooded my space as I sat in meditation and imagined resistance sliding off my body and out of my space. As resistance cleared, pictures appeared and I gained clarity allowing me to open up to the possibility of a new, furry family member. A few months later, we welcomed a puppy into our family which has already provided many happy memories with more to come.

In this example, I looked beyond the resistance energy to see a fear picture that limited me from taking a step. Seeing the picture behind resistance didn't mean we had to then move forward with welcoming a dog. Noticing when you experience resistance and then pausing to look for pictures associated with that energy gives you the opportunity to gain insight and consciously decide how to proceed versus reacting to the resistance energy. A common response to resistance is to shut down or quit. While that might be the best option some of the time, other times investigating further opens up choices. If I had not looked at the resistance I felt initially about the thought of a dog, we most likely would not have gotten a dog. Sometimes seeing means you release the resistance and leave it at that which in this example would have translated to me identifying the fear lurking behind the resistance, letting it go, and moving on without welcoming a dog. Either way, I had discovered and learned more about myself. For our case, it meant I was able to identify the fear and move past it with a dog.

Resistance loves to hide. We see it as fear, anger, frustration, being too busy or even sadness. Recognizing resistance, when and how it creeps into your life, creates an opportunity to navigate each day with more ease. Imagine going down a water slide with no water - ouch! Now add a trickle of water and see yourself gliding all the way down without friction. This is akin to experiencing resistance in your space as well as its elimination. When you clear it, you allow understanding, amusement and ease to take its place. You could still choose to go down a dry waterslide, except why would you when a gentler option exists?

Meditation: Scram resistance! Permission granted!

For this meditation, let's build upon the techniques already presented to go deeper into freeing ourselves energetically so we may
have the permission to create the lives our spirits authentically desire.
By now, you may have a favorite spot for meditating or may enjoy
meditating wherever you find yourself no matter the time or place.
Either way, you are finding what works for you as you develop your
practice. In this meditation, as always, explore and follow what feels
good and resonates with you.

*Close your eyes or soften your gaze as you settle into your body. No-
tice your fingers and toes. Roll your neck and shoulders. Say hello to
your body, giving yourself a deep inhale and exhale as you ground to
the center of the Earth with a grounding cord. Notice the image that
pops up as your grounding cord. Your grounding cord may change each
time you meditate. Let yourself instantly be supported, expanding your
grounding cord to encompass your entire body and the space around
you.*

*Define your space with a protection bubble or filter of your choosing.
Fill in with your energy, imagining and seeing your unique energy cascade in and around your body like the image of rays from your gold
sun or golden rain drops falling from a glittering sky. Pull your attention back behind your eyes to the center of your head and instantly
notice the space you have created for you alone. Let yourself be here -
present, in your body, in this moment, in the center of your head. Let
your body relax and give yourself permission to release.*

*Start right here giving yourself permission to receive insights and
information you are ready to see and have. Notice how your body responds to granting yourself the permission to receive. Do you see any
pictures or words popping up? Letting yourself see however the information presents itself to you.*

Now take a look in your mind's eye at a picture of you when you didn't have permission to feel or act as you did. Maybe you felt shutdown in some way. What are you doing? Who are you with? Where are you located in the picture?

As you see pictures, words, phrases, symbols or colors pop up in your mind's eye, give yourself permission to ask questions and to gather more information. What would it look like to not feel shut down? Then, ask for information about next steps and where to go from here. Give yourself permission to move forward. See what that looks like for you.

As you give yourself permission, notice what is shifting. Continue to breathe, coming back to the center of your head if you drift out. Let your thoughts come up and ground out to the center of the Earth through your supportive grounding cord. If judgment or effort enter, see them and let them pass too.

When we resist something, we allow it to hang around longer. As thoughts pop up in meditation that don't serve you, see them, acknowledge them, and let them go down your grounding cord like bath water down the drain or destroy them. See them blow up like a firework in the night sky or evaporate like morning mist.

When you find yourself working from a place of resistance, imagine yourself effortlessly gliding like a hawk through air or imagine raindrops trickling down your windowpane. Let any resistance slide away from you and your space down your grounding cord. Let your body instantly and effortlessly experience how this non-resistance feels.

Take a few deep breaths as you imagine yourself in this space of non-resistance, seeing resistance leaving your space, energy falling off your body, freeing you up to see what you want to create and to have as your next step. As you release resistance, your breathing might shift. You may notice you have more space in your body for your energy. Continue to breathe as you practice and sit in this space of nonresistance.

As you continue in this meditation, give yourself permission to clear anything (thoughts, energies, beliefs, etc) that might be blocking you consciously or unconsciously. By simply being in this space, practicing non-resistance and setting the intention to release, you clear energy. Allow yourself to be conscious of what you are seeing, intuiting and learning. Let yourself consciously gain insights into your next steps. Take a few more deep breaths. You can come back to this place of permission and non-resistance any time. Once you have created something, you can have it again.

When you are ready, open your eyes and come out of meditation, stretching, yawning, standing, and bringing movement back to your body.

Meditation Tips and Tricks:

- Energy has the potential to move rapidly – you may set the intention to look at something then the pictures appear in rapid succession - that is okay.

- Likewise, sometimes pictures take a moment or two to form - that is okay too.

- Sometimes you don't know exactly what you are resisting or what energy you are clearing, you can still let it go (down your grounding cord or by creating and destroying objects or the image that represents the energy).

- As you practice, you may notice your meditation style evolves as you shift and change.

- Different meditation techniques will resonate for you at different times.

- Give yourself permission to play in meditation – keep it light. Find amusement.

Questions after Meditating:

- Where did you find you were lacking permission?

- Are there places in your life you would like more permission?
- Was it easy to visualize releasing resistance?
- Prior to this meditation, did you know permission and resistance played a part in your life?

6

Chapter 6: When Life Feels Hard

Body, mind, and spirit talk is great when everything feels peachy and is going swimmingly. When life gives you lemons or even worse, you might feel too weary or angry to delve into meditation. How could it possibly help us through dark, excruciating times? For my clients and students, and in my own life, the answer is a resounding yes. Meditation complements other forms of important self-care like therapy, pharmacological interventions, exercise and emotional support too.

Connecting to our body, mind and spirit in meditation provides another avenue of support when tough times arise. Working with energy is not about being perfect, always having the answers and feeling perpetually happy. It's about a willingness to pause, to reflect and to see what might be unfolding. It may not always make sense. Through practicing meditation and tuning in to our intuition, we open up to insights that may help us understand a situation. When something doesn't go well, something throws you off your path, the rug gets pulled out from under you, having a practice to fall back on - a grounding - gives you a base of support. This is why we: meditate, see, know, trust, repeat and practice, practice, practice. When hard times knock us down, our practice exists to catch and buoy us.

Back when I was training for a marathon, as my running team got to know one another, we shared ideas, training tips and strategies. Hearing others' stories is so powerful. We are not intended to be islands. I found myself looking forward to training days for this connection and to hear about what others were doing, how they were feeling and how they handled training and life. While we ran, we talked, we laughed, we coached and counseled each other, we sang, we encouraged and sometimes just breathed together. This builds a strong network and support system.

Learning the value of and the steps to take to create an emotional support system has served me every day since. It takes practice to trust, to welcome others into your life, to allow yourself to be seen as you are and to even just share space with others. Letting others be part of your journey and sharing experiences is a boon and one that can make days not only easier, but a whole lot more fun. My meditation practice opened me up physically, mentally, and spiritually while also, leading me down a path of developing friendships and expanded trust I may have been too busy to notice, see, have or welcome. Stories enrich our lives; shared stories enrich generations.

When something feels wrong, when there is pain, when we suffer from loss, when we are in the middle of a tragedy or hardship, life can feel challenging and hard. Life is constantly throwing us curve balls. It's not about knowing and anticipating every pitch, rather about having a solid base to come back to when you need it. Having a connection to ourselves and others, grounding and neutrality build a foundation. The more in tune you are, the easier to recover when the hard stuff enters and the easier it is to honor what you need during these challenging times.

As we talk about tuning in to body, mind and spirit, be mindful of what you are doing and how you are feeling. Some days you may nail it. Other days, you may feel as though you missed the mark entirely. The good news – you can always press reset and come back to the space you have created. If you have done something once, you can do it again. If you have had a relationship once, you can have another one. If you have made a million dollars once, you can make it again. If you have secured a job, you can get another one, and so on, and so forth. While we are not aiming to have the exact same reality as we had in the past, we create similar and sometimes richer experiences for our futures.

As you practice and grow your awareness, have compassion for yourself and others. We are all here learning and growing at different paces and in different ways. We are all doing what we can with the information we have. If we can find compassion in our hearts for ourselves and for others, because we are all connected, we win. We are already here so let's be here for each other. What I do has an impact on you and vice versa, the waves and tides roll together. As we each tune in individually, we impact the collective.

Through using your meditation practice, you notice and see connections. When you see something, you make sense of it and gain a better understanding of it. Meditation offers a chance to practice seeing and asking questions to reach new depths of knowing. When you are in meditation, ask what are you feeling, what are you noticing, what information is coming up for you. Let yourself see, feel, or experience whatever reveals itself, keeping in mind that there is no right or wrong. Notice the pictures that appear for you.

Developing Your own Intuitive Language

If you feel yourself in meditation drifting to that place of judgment, wanting to decide right versus wrong, good versus bad, come back to your center. As a reminder, you can find your center by resting your attention in the center of your head. This place can become your sanctuary - a place for you to find your space, your voice and your answers. You may have already become very comfortable here.

The center of your head is a place for you to connect with your energy and your information. You can find this place anytime during the day - when you are in meditation or out of meditation. Drawing your attention to the center of your head creates a space for you to connect with neutrality, an energy that moves you out of judgment where it is no longer about right or wrong, good versus bad, rather about the energy and what it looks like and feels like to you. This is the place for clear seeing, a place for you to connect to your clairvoyance, and see your pictures, your insights and receive your intuitive messages. As you practice more and more, you will see more and more, you will understand more and more, and you will read more and more. Much like reading words in a book, the more you practice, the more words you know and understand. The more you meditate and practice reading energy, the easier to know and understand your intuitive or clairvoyant language. Use the center of your head as your platform to dive into seeing and interpreting pictures and energy.

When I started taking meditation and clairvoyant classes, a fellow student described symbols and shapes every time she did a reading. I felt in awe. I saw nothing like what she detailed. She would sketch pictures of triangles, swirls of shapes, and lots of colors with her words. She told them in a way that painted a picture for the person she read and they understood it. I loved hearing her read because the pictures she would describe were so different from what I saw. It took me a little bit to realize that the difference didn't mean better. She read pictures differently than I did. As we continued reading together, I realized I saw the same energy she read in different pictures. My pictures sometimes came through as landscapes and other times as pictures with subtitles. I would see it like a movie where she would see and intuit in shapes and symbols. To her the shapes and symbols all meant something. To me, the scenes and snapshots of pictures meant something. We arrived at the same place through different means. She saw a series of squares inside each other getting smaller and smaller while I saw a person stepping inside a box, inside another box, inside another box. The energy of the picture translated to feeling confined and boxed in, stuck and limited. We both recognized the same energy in the form of different pictures illustrating similar meanings.

My classmate showed and reminded me that we all see and read differently. There is not a one size fits all or a one right way. There is only your way that works best for you. When you hone your ability and let your pictures, sounds or feelings guide you, reading and intuiting become easy. Your only job remains to tune in and receive the information and insights. It seems abstract at first and, possibly, even incomprehensible. A second hand description helps, however not as much as the firsthand experience of jumping in and looking through your own meditation and energy work practice.

Developing your own intuitive or psychic language is a matter of paying attention. When you feel called to wear a green shirt, reflect at the end of the day as to what unfolded. Was it a particularly challenging day? A day full of growth and changes? Was it happy and light? Is there a theme or a feeling that accompanies this color? How about when you notice the same symbol or animal reappear with frequency or hear a similar phrase over the span of a few days? Reflect on what was happening when you saw or heard the symbol or phrase. Use a journal to take notes and track your observations over time to see how your meditation is changing or a pattern of similar images and messages might be evolving on a certain trajectory.

In meditation, ask what different colors mean or represent to you then see what pictures pop up in your mind's eye. What do these pictures convey to you? As you ask questions from a place of curiosity, the information reveals itself. Let yourself explore while suspending the urge to judge right or wrong and remain in the center of your head, working from neutrality and non-judgment. Again, if judgment or resistance come in, simply return to what we practiced in the resistance meditation to let it flow away and then reset in the center of your head.

As I have done more and more readings over the years, different colors will come up in readings which will almost always prompt the question: what does that color mean? I ask clients and students to decide what colors mean to them and how they feel in their space. Nothing beats exploring for yourself how the colors feel, look, and resonate with you. While there is no time and space when it comes to spirit, there is no substitute for taking the time on the physical level to sit, meditate, and look for yourself at how different colors, symbols, words, ideas, and pictures feel and resonate with you. My color key works for me in my practice, but may not for you. This is why I recommend developing your own while also being patient and gentle with yourself.

Throw out any previous notions of what meditation must be that you have collected from television shows, books or even your own experience. For instance, time spent in meditation does not have to take hours. Make meditation work for you. Be open to exploration and finding what things look like and feel like to you. The amount of time is not the important piece. The discovery, the ability to see yourself, to know what something means to you and to develop your own shorthand of communication are the goals. Then when you are confronted with energies that don't feel good or belong in your space, you recognize them, feel them, see them, and intuit them. Then use your techniques such as grounding, creating and destroying or filling with your energy to clear them out.

Much like learning how to read as a child takes practice, learning how to interpret or "read" your intuition, the pictures and images that pop up in meditation, does too. Another key ingredient and technique to foster success in developing this ability is amusement as we have explored a bit already. Have fun and make it work for you whether that means meditating while you lie down, taking a walking meditation approach or meditating in short increments multiple times a day or week. It is about you learning and zeroing in on what works for you in order to achieve a better sense of understanding and clarity for the information to come to you in a way that you use to navigate your life.

I felt incredibly nervous in the first professional reading I ever did. Unsure of what would surface and if I would find the words to convey the pictures adequately to the person, I had to trust my abilities and my mediation foundation to guide me. As we started the reading, a purple butterfly kept flying through the pictures popping up from my mind's eye. While I don't remember any of the other pictures from this reading, I will never forget the purple butterfly because it would not leave until I mentioned it. I resisted mentioning it for the first several minutes of the reading. After I read the picture of the butterfly and spoke it out loud, it did not return for the rest of the reading. I gave myself permission to see what was happening in front of me in the pictures. When I did, something magical and healing happened.

As the reading ended, my client, who had remained relatively quiet during the reading, shared with me that she had been adopted and the one thing her birth mother had given her was a pin of a purple butterfly. She knew the purple butterfly was a message to her - not for me to necessarily understand or know - a picture she understood immediately and was tremendously significant. She was in awe and couldn't believe the picture I had relayed.

That picture gave a healing to the client as well as reminded me of the power of seeing and sharing pictures. The pictures may not always make sense at the moment. However, the more we practice, the more we are willing to look and ask questions, the easier it is to see and allow meaningful information to show up. As you see and read more, your ability to understand and intuit strengthens as you allow the space and permission for this to happen.

Your practice offers a foundation, a grounding, to move through the ups and downs, to navigate life without losing your center and your connection to yourself. Meditation, seeing and reading energy becomes a tool to find a different vantage point and to discover insights along your path, as well as for others if you choose.

Meditation: Developing Your Intuition

As your meditation practice grows, recognize some techniques might come easier than others or feel better to practice at times. Give yourself grace and patience as you practice. Why not sprinkle in a little amusement? This meditation will tie together the techniques we have gone over thus far and prompt you to discover more about yourself and your intuitive language.

As you settle into your meditation space, close your eyes, give yourself a grounding cord of your choosing, see your energy fall in your space and fill you in with your unique energy however that looks to you. Take a few deep breaths and notice how your body is feeling. Check in with yourself. How are you feeling? What are you noticing and seeing?

Pull back into the center of your head and let yourself sit in the space you have created for you and you alone. As you take another deep breath or two, give your body permission to release and relax. Let any tension or stress in your body, mind or space exit through your grounding cord down to the center of the Earth, and notice that you can be in your space, in your body, safe, grounded and full of your energy. Let yourself be present in this moment.

As you create and destroy bubbles or the object of your choice, notice any resistance creeping into your space and practice non-resistance, imagining your body as a slide and any resistance slipping right off your body like going down a slide.

Take another deep breath as you notice what you are seeing. What are you intuiting? See pictures or information popping up. What do you need to know right now? What insights or information are available to you right now? Is there a decision you are looking to make or something you would like more information on before taking a next step? If so, ask yourself for a picture relating to that upcoming decision or situation. What do you see? Allow yourself to tune in to the pictures in front of you, the colors, shapes or symbols that appear or perhaps messages heard or intuited.

Working from the center of your head allows you to see the information without judgment. It's climbing the tree to spot your friends below versus being in the middle of the crowd not able to find them. You are creating a space to receive information and insights as well as have greater perspective. See the pictures, the words, the colors and the symbols as they appear and allow yourself to sit with the information they hold. Recognize it might not all make sense in the moment but may at a future time. Be in the space of meditation, tuning in and noticing. Asking questions and letting the pictures appear. Take a deep breath and continue to let yourself practice seeing.

As you practice more and more, you will start to develop your own language, an understanding of how your intuition communicates with you. You will know what different colors and symbols mean to you in time.

As you meditate, continue breathing and asking questions - be curious and notice what pops up, what you see and what the images mean to you. There is no right or wrong. This is a space to learn, to intuit, to grow and to expand your awareness. If you leave the center of your head or get distracted, no problem, create and destroy, pop a bubble or two, and come right back to the space. There is no time and space when it comes to energy. Move in and out of this meditation as you choose.

Find your amusement and let yourself enjoy the moment. Be present, be grounded and be curious. Continue breathing, expanding and contracting with each inhale and exhale. Notice the pictures appearing from your mind's eye. See for yourself what energy is unfolding in front of you. Let yourself be in this space for as long as it feels good to you discovering what pictures, images, colors, shapes and symbols mean for you.

When you feel ready, come out of meditation by creating and destroying another object, rose or popping a bubble, open your eyes, yawn or stretch as you move back into your body.

Meditation Tips and Tricks:

- If you have a tendency to fall asleep during meditation, that's okay. You might notice that as you practice, you stay awake longer. Alternatively, every time you look at a certain topic, you could fall asleep. If so, there might be more to investigate around this topic.

- Your meditation and intuitive language will grow and change as your practice grows and changes.

- While it's great to talk about meditation with friends/partners, comparisons don't work when it comes to meditation. Everyone's practice is different. Share insights and ideas while refraining from judgment or attempting to match each other.

Question after Meditating:

- What colors or symbols appeared for you? What have you discovered different colors or symbols mean to you?

- Did any themes or repeated images emerge for you?

- Are you able to give yourself permission to see in your own time and space?

- Which techniques are resonating most right now for you?

Chapter 7: Integration

Life is fast. We are often reacting to circumstances, to what is happening around us and to what needs to be done in the moment. Taking time to check in with our body, mind and spirit and to meditate makes a world of difference in how we experience every day. A bit of willingness, a splash of mindfulness, and a dash of amusement go a long way on the road to experiencing, having and creating integration of the body, mind and spirit.

The power of having a heightened awareness to our body, mind and spirit, is that we then receive information faster. We know ourselves better. We are able to have our answers more quickly. The power of integration is that body, mind, and spirit then work in harmony, in rhythm, allowing us to flow from one to the other. It's in the flow that our life unfolds with ease; our path emerges individually suited for each one of us. It doesn't mean everything is always easy, always happy, always perfect. It means that when we are flowing with our intuition, we can recognize how that feels and so also recognize when we are not in alignment to then move back into the flow with as little stress, tension and anxiety as possible.

Getting to this place requires tuning in, showing up, looking, asking, speaking, listening and receiving – practicing our meditation and energy work techniques every day. Integration of body, mind, spirit, doesn't always happen smoothly. Even as we integrate, there are bumps along the road. We might completely miss something our body is telling us; we might spend all day in our thoughts; we might forget to listen to our spirit for a week. Yet, as we practice, as we hone our ability to tune in, we inevitably connect to our path, which feeds into finding our purpose and knowing our authentic selves.

I had the fortune of stumbling into meditation. I had started on the mindfulness journey a bit in college and graduate school when exploring and reading books on the topic. I had always believed in the concept of expecting the best to get the best, that our habits define us and the like. When I delved deeper and found meditation, I grew into a better version of myself. Meditation became a habit that continues to serve me beyond my understanding.

After moving to Chicago for graduate school and only knowing a couple of people, I lucked into a spiritual book club meeting held at a yoga studio. The owner of the studio started the book club and she and I became fast friends to my delight. She suggested I check out a meditation class, which led to many insights and discoveries. It was as if someone handed me the key to what I didn't realize I had been searching for and the path to uncovering all my answers. I found a space that I could come to visit, and stay as long as I liked anytime, anywhere. It was magic to me. Meditation became my best tool for handling stress, ups and downs and basically all that goes along with life.

I loved meditating while on the train, in the beautiful parks, along the waterfront, or in my small studio apartment. From meditation (spirit), I deepened my yoga practice and became a yoga instructor (body), then branched into a more in depth knowledge of meditation (mind) which all came together to lead to a greater understanding of myself, my journey, my purpose and even went a long way in improving my own self-care.

My body, mind, and spirit alignment took center stage. during this time in Chicago. Life decisions definitely became easier. When

I met my now husband, I knew the instant I laid eyes on him he was the one. It wasn't love at first sight like in fairy tales, rather a knowing, and a certainty that came out of getting to know myself through my meditation practice of grounding, working from the center of my head (neutrality), and bringing in amusement, asking myself how I felt and noticing what thoughts I had about different aspects of my life and connecting to spirit, landed in me knowing myself.

It's not so important whether you stumble into alignment from the bottom up, top down, middle out (body, mind or spirit; spirit, mind or body; mind, body or spirit). The important piece is the knowledge – tuning in and seeing, getting the answers, asking clarifying questions, being curious and paying attention. Meditation is a way to make connections with these aspects in order to know ourselves fully and deeply. Having the certainty in yourself, knowing yourself so truly, changes how you experience life. It doesn't mean you don't ever change your mind, can't be swayed toward a different way of thinking, get everything right or know everything. Rather it lends itself to adjusting as needed as you move through your day, to flexibility in thinking, and to willingness to explore and grow.

As we talk about integration, we might naturally aim for some sort of equal balance between body, mind and spirit. While that sounds like a natural goal, I caution setting up that expectation. We are constantly evolving. What might feel like balance one minute, might be completely off the next. The common notion of balance is equal parts in all sections. If we were to then balance body, mind and spirit for integration purposes, we would spend a third in each every day. And yet, that is not exactly how life works. When it comes to balance, energetically speaking, it can take many forms. We might need to devote more time to the body one week followed by a week of spirit time. We may have a job that requires more mental work than physical work, yet feel balanced after an hour in the gym. We are not aiming for equal parts in terms of time spent in each. We are seeking what feels good, what looks good, what is called for and needed in the moment we find ourselves. It's a dynamic system requiring flexibility and our own knowing and trusting of what we require..

Sleep restores the body, mind and spirit in a way nothing else can come close. During sleep, we process, we assimilate and we integrate with little resistance. Sleep is a time to bring body, mind, and spirit together effortlessly. During sleep, we explore without judgment as we let our body rest, our mind relax and our spirit soar. Sleep helps integrate all we see and learn during our day and in our meditations.

During sleep, we often spend a portion of the time unconsciously processing the events of the day or stresses on our minds or hearts before moving on to more insightful dreams. Our dreams represent our growth, what we want to see or manifest. It is in our dreams that we envision ourselves doing things and then are able to create them in the physical, tangible world. If you want to do something, dream about it. Dreaming moves energy from the spirit to the physical body where visions manifest.

I love to meditate before I go to sleep, to set my dream space up for success. I use meditation to release my stresses and tensions from the day and to let go of whatever I might hold onto consciously or unconsciously from the day. I do this as I prepare for my sleep and my dreams. Initially, I used to fall asleep shortly into my meditation. As I have practiced, I now stay awake for the duration of my meditation before drifting off to sleep, as I want.

My meditation allows me to integrate the information I take in during the day, what I see and notice, and gives me a space to consciously look at and process what happened earlier. As I got more seasoned in my meditation practice, I started to notice trends, themes and developed my own language as to what different things meant to me.

In addition to meditation, writing in a journal served as a resource to track themes and shifts occurring. Through jotting down notes, goals and aspirations, I began to consciously increase my awareness of my ability to manifest. Through looking at the energy of things in meditation and taking notes, I could see correlations between what unfolded and what I intuited during meditation.

I then began utilizing my sleep and dreams as another avenue to see and gain insights, to set my intentions. As I knew my body, mind and spirit more fully through meditation and tuning in, I set intentions for what I wanted to know or see during my dreams. I used my sleep time as a chance to play and explore. I set an intention before going to sleep, sometimes writing it down, sometimes making a mental note and then noticed what came up as I slept and dreamt. Much like meditation, I picked up on themes and trends in my dreams too, many times validating my intentions by providing me with insights and next steps.

When you open up to your information in your dream space, no limits exist to what can unfold. There is no shortage of information to see and discover each and every day through this nocturnal energy work. By first tuning in to our body, mind and spirit, then practicing meditation, we create space to know more about ourselves and our path, or unlock our ability to read for others. There is a lot to know within ourselves. Meditation and dreams offer a path to all there is to discover.

Meditation: Setting your Sleep Space

Gaining insights into both your waking and sleeping moments is a way to propel your meditation practice to the next level. This meditation will walk you through setting your space to begin to work with intuiting and reading energy in your dreams.

Take a deep breath as you settle into your body and space. Close your eyes, if it feels right for you, soften your gaze, and find your grounding, your balance and your protection bubble. Be in the center of your head, the center of your space, defining your space by your energy, your protection bubble and your grounding cord. Let your entire body be supported, releasing any energy you are ready to let go of and filling in with your unique vibration. Notice your energy in your space and let your energy be healing to you.

As you clear out your day, you can imagine a picture representing your day out in front of you and blow it up by seeing it explode like a firework or dissolve like sugar in water signifying it has come and gone. Create a picture of your day and destroy it. Let it go. Create and destroy. Use a rose, an image or a color to represent your day, and release it from your space. Ground it out after you destroy it, knowing that any energy that was caught up in your day that belongs to you will return to you. Your energy will always find its way back to you. Also give yourself permission to release other people's energy that might be lingering in your space still caught up from the day. Clear out any energy that you don't need by setting the intention to and sending the energy down your grounding cord.

Notice thoughts and feelings while also practicing non-resistance as they move through your body and space. See pictures popping up and gain insights from what is unfolding. If you drift from the center of your head, jump right back, no problem.

Set your intention for your sleep and dream time. What do you want to dream about, learn or see? What insights would you like to have? What messages would you like to receive? Who would you like to dream about or see in your dreams? Let yourself paint the picture or make the list. Jot down or read your intentions to yourself. As you set this space, imagine running neutral gold energy through your sleep and dream space like a ribbon, using whatever gold color appears. Lace your dreams with this neutral vibration of gold. Set your intention for a restful sleep, a productive sleep, a restorative sleep, whatever sleep you would like, giving yourself permission to have it without effort.

Take a deep breath or two as you set your intentions, see your intentions and work the energy of your sleep and dream space. Let yourself be grounded and safe, tune in to your sleep space. When you are ready and have set your sleep space, come out of meditation. If you are heading to sleep, you might want to end the meditation with your eyes open for a moment rather than standing up and stretching your body. Use the space you have set for yourself and drift off into sleep.

Meditation Tips and Tricks:

- When doing a sleep meditation, you can be laying down and ready for bed.

- If you fall asleep the first few times while practicing this meditation, that's okay.

- Intentions are powerful – play with setting intentions for other aspects of your day and life. Remember intentions work best when they are about and for you, not others.

- Let your meditation practice grow with you.

- Use journaling as an aid throughout your meditation practice. Designate a journal for your dreams and/or your meditation notes.

Questions after Meditating:

- Take note when you wake up about how you slept. Did you notice a difference in your sleep and how you feel the next day versus nights when you don't set yourself up intentionally for sleep with a meditation?

- How does it feel to ground before bed?

- In this meditation, we used neutral gold energy as opposed to your unique gold energy. Was that easy to visualize? How did it feel to you?

- Where else might you want to play with and work with neutral gold (i.e. swirling it through your work/school day, lacing it through your house, office or car)?

8

Chapter 8: Intuition to Clairvoyance

Growth periods happen throughout our lives and yet somehow after we hit puberty, they are not as widely accepted. When we need extra sleep and aren't a teenager (or dealing with a legitimate health concern), people judge and ask, "What's wrong?" The answer we should feel proud to respond with is, "Nothing, I'm growing!"

In my house, when things feel intense and everyone is changing (either physically, emotionally, spiritually or all three), we call it a growth period. A growth period is when we, as individuals, become more capable and yet, some growth periods can feel totally the opposite. They are not always linear in form.

When our children grow, we celebrate. We have parties, we text our friends ("she took her first steps!") and we announce to everyone with beaming pride. When the growth periods become less about the physical ("He grew 4 inches in a year!") and more emotional or spiritual ("I decided I don't have to live with the limiting belief that I can't be as smart as my sister"), we don't tend to celebrate them. We sometimes even hide them. We forget to validate how they help us continue along on our authentic life path, and also help those around us grow too.

When we make a change, others must adjust in some way, even subtly. When we take a step, it ripples outward. Likewise, when someone around us changes, we have to adjust. We are all connected.

Changes and adjustments are simple to see when they are on the physical plane. For example, you do construction on your house and move the front door. When people come over, they have to enter at a different point. They make the change. They adjust.

When shifts are on the mind or spirit level, the adjustments can feel a bit more uncomfortable and less tangible making them harder to address or acknowledge for others. When you let go of a thought or idea that might be holding you back, energetically things shift for you. The best friend that also held the same idea but may not feel it is limiting them so do not desire a change or might not be ready to take the step you did at this time might resist your adjustment. It may not be conscious that you shifted in a way they weren't ready to change, and yet something might feel off for them and you. This is common but we don't often see people discussing or describing these kinds of experiences in everyday life.

As an energy worker, I would observe this occurring and intentionally share with a friend or family member something along the lines of "I cleared a big picture from my space today. I could tell that it was holding me back from doing what I want in my life. I see you are holding a similar picture but I am not quite sure you feel the need or are ready to make such a shift yet or at all. That is up to you. However, if you pick up on the fact that my energy feels or looks different, I wanted you to understand why." From an energy perspective this is exactly how to describe an intangible shift that leads to an inner growth period and when those around you may feel off or even bothered in some way related to your leap.

This type of growth often gets interpreted by others more like "Something is different with her. I'm not sure what but I don't think I like it. I am not sure we are still going to be friends and I'm not sure why. Just something feels different." Or "She's different. Oh, well. Let's ignore it and continue on business as usual."

When we can notice, see, tune in and recognize these growths and shifts in ourselves and others, we then hold space to accept, adjust and communicate about them, life gets easier. The little differences that went unnamed or misunderstood get clarified. Our language changes – we become energy workers (which is to say people who acknowledge energy, see and recognize it moving and shifting around them). We become beings that flow with our own energy and can also see and recognize the energy of others and energies in and around our space.

We speak about the unseen – we tune in to the fact that just because we can't see it in our physical reality, doesn't mean it's not true. Remember our elephants from the beginning? Energy is all around us, all the time. Energy stirred up in Kansas ripples out to North Dakota – even though we can't see it in the air but on an energy level it is there. We energetically can feel it and tune in to it. When we have the awareness that the energy from somewhere else might impact us, we can separate out and divert it so that we may continue on our path and in our own energy.

If something doesn't belong to us, it's difficult to solve. We can feel overwhelmed when energies that don't belong to us get mixed in with our energy. This is where all of our techniques serve us so well. As we ground, pull back into the center of our heads, and metaphorically sprinkle amusement into our space and our perspective, we create room for clarity, for understanding and for clear seeing. In that, truth emerges, the path is revealed; we are renewed, rejuvenated and our world re-created. Body, mind and spirit move in concert with each other.

To get to this place of integration and clear seeing takes patience and practice as I've shared. We are all in a body to learn, to grow, to get better, to see and to enjoy this life. Lucky for us all, we have different paths and different lessons to experience. Our paths may cross with others to create beautiful memories and connections. Likewise, sometimes our paths cross and produce conflict or trauma. We all came here to heal and grow, in some way, some fashion.

Healing looks different to everyone. What is healing to one might not be healing to another. An experience for one might produce a growth outcome for one person, while creating unbearable trauma for the next. The goal is not one size fits all, rather it is to know what is healing to you. One of the most powerful things to come out of my journey thus far is to know how to heal myself. Some days the healing looks like a walk with a friend, sometimes it looks like a quiet meditation or sometimes it's takeout on a busy Tuesday night. What the healing is doesn't matter as much as knowing and trusting yourself on what you need.

It has been said that all healing is self-healing and that healing one's self is healing all. When you take time to develop your intuition, to know yourself through tuning into your body, mind and spirit; when you give yourself permission to receive insights and information, to honor the hard stuff along with the easier stuff; when you develop your communication with yourself through meditation, through your dreams and to honor your path, you are not only healing yourself, you are healing those around you too. You help the collective. When one takes a step forward, we all do. When one wins, we all win.

To do my part in this collective growth, I rely on my meditation techniques such as grounding, working with my own unique energy and non-resistance daily to support me as a wife, mother, daughter, sister, friend, neighbor, employee and just as myself. I still make mistakes, forget my practice, get frustrated, second-guess, yell and stumble at times. I am human, practicing meditation and looking at energy every day. Using meditation, intuition and honing my ability to see and read energy enabled me to better understand my direction and purpose. I have gotten faster at identifying opportunities and trained myself to recognize energetic messages.

Intuition is getting a sense of something and following it. It's the gut feeling that pushed you to go left instead of right where you avoided three hours of traffic. It's the knowing of the messages coming from our pictures in meditation. Intuition is a valuable resource and an important tool. It is a bridge to diving into and developing your clairvoyance, your ability to see energy clearly, more fully. Intuition is middle school if clairvoyance were high school. As you gain confidence in your intuition, you naturally want to see and know more. Clairvoyance is seeing the energy of the intuitive thought or feeling that led you to adjust your course of action. When you intuit, you may not know the why. When you look at the energy though, you can go that one step further to clairvoyance and ask to see the why. Through meditation we can use our techniques to see the energy of what is, what was and even what is potentially to come as well as the why of it all.

When you can see something, you can create it, you can have it. When you work from the center of your head, from the space of neutrality and non-judgment, you see and create. Your ticket to manifesting the life, the dreams and all that your heart desires is working from and within your clairvoyant space, that exact space you have created in this book.

Grounding, running energy, filling in with your energy, defining your own meditative space, having your attention in the center of your head and releasing resistance are all meditation techniques that foster moving into and developing your clairvoyance even further. Using these energetic techniques in meditation clears your body and space of energies that do not belong to you. When you have your energy in your space, you create the room to see what is yours and what isn't. That is key to reading and understanding the energy you are experiencing and in turn, seeing and knowing your truth, or that for others if you are reading for them.

Most of us would notice if we came home from work one day and found our neighbors couch in our living room. Yet when it comes to energy, we are not as aware of what we take on that actually belongs to others. We unknowingly absorb our coworker's energy and walk around for days feeling out of sorts without realizing why. If we think of our energetic field (sometimes referred to as an aura, a space surrounding us 360 degrees and about a foot to three feet out) like our living room, we basically are walking around with someone else's couch in our aura. We may have lived with our neighbor's couch in our space for months and probably very uncomfortably so. Imagine removing the couch and returning it to its rightful owner. See how much more room you have for you and your furnishings. They fit your space perfectly with style and comfort that speak to you.

Taking your intuition to the next step of clairvoyance (from acting on gut feelings or hunches to seeing clearly and reading energy in the form of pictures, words, symbols, colors and shapes from the mind's eye) means seeing when someone else's energetic couch is taking up residence in your space. It is moving from feeling to consciously seeing and naming through knowing your intuitive language. We would say something or do something if our neighbor's couch was in our living room without our consent, and yet, we rarely act when we have someone else's energy sitting in our space. Why is that? It is simple, we don't recognize it as foreign energy. We go through our days oblivious to the energy we have taken on or are holding in our body and space even though it may not feel good.

As mainstream as meditation is, it still isn't something most of us feel comfortable talking about with everyone in our lives. It probably isn't the talk around the water cooler at most offices. This impacts all of us because we are not trained, taught or encouraged to speak up when our energy feels off, if we see we have taken on something that isn't ours, or if we are seeing the energy of something that needs addressing. Instead, we ignore the couch. We sit down and attempt to make it work or we get angry without knowing why; we lash out, we say things we regret, all because we didn't see that someone else's couch had invaded our space. And to share with others why we felt off still feels taboo in many situations.

If only we could see the energetic couch as soon as it appeared, name it and clear it. That is the power of using your clairvoyant space every day and working with energy every day. It's not about being perfect. The couches will still appear. As long as you live with and interact with other humans on a regular basis, you will be subject to feeling all the human emotions. As you hone the ability to see, you gain strategies to handle, cope, work with, and clear the day-to-day challenges.

I would love to say that I get it right 100% of the time - that after almost twenty years of practicing meditation and energy work, I never get frustrated, tired, sick or have an off day, that rouge energetic couches never slip in and go unnoticed in my space. Alas, I live in the real world and am a human being susceptible to all the fallible tendencies that go along with that - meaning, I sometimes get angry, yell, make mistakes, feel sad, fail and get upset at others. Developing your ability to see energy doesn't translate into always feeling balanced and happy. It does, however, lend itself to more quickly realizing when things are off. You already have the path mapped out for returning to center and for clearing situations before they root.

To ensure I don't drift too far off my path, I consciously practice looking at energy every day. Meditating and reading energy is like anything else: in order for it to become easier and a daily habit, it requires regular practice. For the majority of people, situations or decisions I encounter throughout my day, I either read the energy as it unfolds in real time or I take the time to review it later via my meditation practice at the end of every day. Before my feet hit the floor each morning, my grounding cord is refreshed and in place. Then, I end my day with a brand new grounding cord and fill my space with my own unique gold color or the color that resonates with me at that moment. I have practiced this for years to the point that if I don't start and end my days this way, I can tell the difference. I have noticed too that whenever I ground, I am reminded to take a deep breath. The combination of the grounding and the deep breath feel like an instant healing and resetting. My body unwinds, my mind clears and my spirit smiles.

Clairvoyance (seeing energy, sometimes referred to as psychic ability) is not a ticket to knowing everything that is going to happen, like exactly how or all the details on the why. The word psychic conjures up the notion of someone who knows exactly what the future holds, whereas looking at the energy of something in meditation brings forth possibilities. I intuit next steps and see the potential that exists. Naming these doesn't necessarily mean something is going to happen. It fosters the space for possibilities to come into being or unfold. What I or others choose to do with this knowledge is based on our own freewill as it should be.

If you were in line for a promotion and came to me for a reading, for example, I would look at the energy of the job, the promotion and the other people in the office. I might tell you that energetically it looks like it is lining up or maybe that there is also something else for you down the pike somewhere else. I did a reading once where that very similar thing happened. A client came back to update me after I had done a reading on his career and next steps. The job had shifted and something unexpected had opened up. The reading gave him the confidence and patience to let things unfold as they needed to, which is often the power of reading energy. It is not about controlling the outcome or ensuring things are going to go one way.

None of us have that much control. The power is in highlighting how and where the energy is flowing.

When we go with that energetic flow, things open up. Reading the energy from a place of neutrality allows you to see the space(s) lining up and, potentially, move into them with more ease and less stress or resistance. Another client asked me to read whether she would receive a job offer for a position she had interviewed. I saw that she would get an offer as it looked like the potential employer had already decided they wanted her to come work for them. In the time it took for her to receive the job offer, she discovered something about her personal health that made her decide to stay with her present employer. If the job offer we knew was coming had arrived as quickly as she had originally hoped, it would have caused distress when she got the news of her personal health situation. Knowing the job offer was energetically on its way offered her patience in waiting for it to arrive on the physical level and then created ease when she needed to change things up and not take the job after all. In seeing the energy, she was able to find patience and trust in the process.

Moving into the center of your head to read the picture associated with your intuition ensures neutrality (you aren't being swayed one way or another) and that you see possible next steps versus following blindly. As mentioned, seeing and reading energy from the center of your head takes practice. You can avoid potentially difficult situations by seeing the possibilities that exist instead of working towards something that may not be available right now. Everything has an energy. You can look at and read the energy of everything from what to have for dinner to what job to accept to what major to study to what name to give your dog to where to live.

Making clairvoyance and reading pictures part of your everyday life takes little more than the willingness to spend time each day looking and asking questions of what pictures you notice and see in meditation. After a while, curiosity drives your practice. I got curious about what happened, why it happened, and what the energy of it meant. I wanted to see, know and understand what was unfolding in my life.

I don't retain details of what I read for others because it is not my information. Occasionally I will remember a particularly poignant picture though. I recall one reading where I saw frogs raining from the sky onto the person. After the reading, she informed me that frogs were her favorite animal and she always had them around her and looked for them. I couldn't tell you anything else about that reading. We don't hold on to other people's details for long because the information does not belong to us. You might remember your best friend's birthday and their phone number; however, you most likely don't remember the exact time their first child was born or the square footage of their house. It simply isn't your information to keep. The same goes for reading pictures and energy for others.

Reading energy is not about predicting the future or knowing everything that is about to happen. Reading energy is about knowing yourself, your space, and seeing your information and your answers. When you see it for yourself, you often move through your own challenges faster and with less effort. It doesn't mean you won't get stuck from time to time or need assistance. It usually means that when you feel stuck, you will recognize it and know who to ask for help from faster than before. You will be able to see how to get out of being stuck.

I seek guidance and help from other practitioners to assist me to see angles into my own information that I may be too close to see at times. Honing your clairvoyant ability does not make you an island; rather it helps you find your tribe. When you see yourself, you see others. When you see others, they see you. Your relationships may shift and change as you embark on your clairvoyant journey. Your energy will move and grow as you look within and see yourself, your truths, and come to know your energy clearly. You will clear out old energy from your space and find your body, mind and spirit shifting in potentially unexpected ways.

As I journeyed into consciously developing my clairvoyant space, I moved, switched my graduate school major, broke up with someone, met my future husband, changed jobs about three times and ran a marathon. It was quite a growth period, a time of me becoming more fully who I was and wanted to be. It felt freeing and also uncertain at times. Everyone's journey is unique as everyone's energy is unique. As you take your next steps into developing your clairvoyant space, consciously know that your energy will shift and change sparking growth in yourself and those around you. Some of it may catch you off guard, some of it may be welcomed change and some of it may create stress as things play out. Hang in there! You can always go back to your meditation basics: a grounding cord, taking a deep breath and filling your space with your energy. Use this foundation as your cornerstone to taking your next steps, falling back on your meditation techniques to support you whenever needed.

Meditation: On Seeing

This meditation focuses on opening your clairvoyant space, your ability to see more deeply into the why and the possibilities that exist. Use this meditation as a template to look at other ideas, opportunities, areas of growth and anything that peaks your curiosity.

When you feel ready, close your eyes and give yourself a new grounding cord. Connect your body to the center of the Earth, creating a channel to release anything you are ready to let go of in this moment. As you take a deep breath or two, consciously let your attention rest behind your eyes in the center of your head. Imagine and see your energy around you. Let your unique vibration shine and rain down in your body and space. Let your energy be a healing to you as you create this space for yourself.

From this grounded place, create a picture from your mind's eye. Ask to see a picture of what you are feeling right now, what energy you are noticing in your life or any other question that pops into your mind. Let yourself explore what you experience right now. Look at a picture of the energy around you. Let yourself see. Notice you can look at anything, anytime, anywhere.

See pictures pop in front of you as if you are looking out at a movie screen. Stay in the center of your head, the place for neutrality and nonjudgment as the pictures appear and unfold. You can imagine it like opening up a picture book. See images in front of you. As you are doing this, you are creating space to see, to look, to be clairvoyant. Anytime you take a moment to explore the energy of something, you create space. When you give something space, it grows.

Pick a topic and look at the energy of it. See it as pictures, colors, shapes and symbols. Remember, this is about developing your intuitive and clairvoyant language. There is no right or wrong.

From the center of your head, create a picture out in front of you of your body and space. See yourself. Is there energy that belongs to someone else in your space? Ask to see a picture. See how the pictures change when you ask. Maybe energy that isn't yours appears as a certain color or symbol. See what happens in the picture as you ask questions. Give yourself permission to see your energy and what your energy looks like to you.

Knowing your energy and what your energy looks like makes it easier to know yourself. As you fill in with your energy, see how the picture of you shifts. Notice if the energy that appeared that isn't yours changes or releases as you fill in with your energy.

You can do this with any aspect of your life. Settle into meditation and take a look. Ask questions. Take yourself on a journey to what you want to create, have and manifest in your life. Use this clairvoyant space to visualize. Once you can see something, you can create it and have it. Practice being in this space to see - this space to not only see, to also gain a greater understanding and awareness. As you practice, you discover your language and what different colors, symbols, pictures and energies mean to you. Stay here as long as you like looking, noticing and exploring what pops up on your movie screen from your mind's eye.

When you are ready, open your eyes and come out of meditation. Wiggle your fingers and your toes as you come back to your body.

Meditation Tips and Tricks:

- Use your meditation time to look at what you want to have and create and even to see what is open to you right now that you might not have noticed.

- Meditation is a great tool to use to manifest in your life: if you see it, you can create it.

- If it feels challenging to look at different aspects of what you want, what you are handling or the energy of a situation, that is okay. Take a break and come back to the meditation later. Honor what you need as you embark on this journey of using your intuition and clairvoyance.

- Meditation is a great way to reset if every feeling unsettled too!

Questions after Meditating:

- How might accessing your intuition and clairvoyance help you on a day-to-day basis?

- Are there goals you wish to manifest that meditation and clear seeing could help you accomplish? If so, what are they?

Chapter 9: Programming

We are conditioned at a young age to follow the rules. We go to school and are taught to raise our hands and wait to be called on to ask a question, to follow the leader, and to listen quietly when someone else is speaking. The list goes on and on. Some of us follow the rules without question. Some of us follow the rules only after some debate about their merits. Some of us make a point not to follow the rules until we have decided they work for us on our terms or not at all regardless of the consequences. Our rule following behaviors help us see how easily we are programmed.

I tended to be a rule follower. On the bus in 1st grade, classmates were throwing around a tin foil ball from someone's lunch. They would toss it up and it would land in someone's lap and so on. Harmless, right? Then, it landed in my lap. I didn't know what to do. My programming said don't throw things on a bus. However, everyone was participating. I decided to join so I stood up and tossed the tin foil ball in the air to the kids a few rows back. It was a rainy day and I was wearing my ruby red raincoat to school. The bus driver looked up the moment the ball left my grasp, pointed his finger in the mirror and said "You, in the red coat, see me when we get to the school." When we arrived, everyone filed off the bus, except for me. I waited and went to see the driver who gave me a lecture about not throwing objects on a bus, especially while it was in transit.

It was then I learned that breaking rules was not my forte. I am the kid that will get caught.

In third grade, my friend sitting at her desk next to me asked a question during a quiz. Not thinking, I whispered back to her. I don't remember what she asked me or if it even related to the quiz. All I remember is my teacher keeping us both inside at recess and lecturing us on cheating. Why did I answer my friend? I knew not to talk during quizzes!

Rules exist everywhere. We are programmed from an early age to follow them. We create societies with rules and mores. If there were no rules like staying on the right side of the road or obeying the speed limit and no one programmed to follow the rules, driving across town could be dangerous.

The challenge is to know which rules work for you, or rather, which programming aligns with you. Knowing the programming that works for you is important for your growth and self-realization. I learned early on that if I broke the rules, it would not work in my favor. As I embarked on my meditation and clairvoyant journey, I delved into programming to look at how these early experiences and others influenced my perspective.

Through self-exploration and investigation, I have come to know my own set of programs. Looking at ourselves from the lens of how we are programmed to think, be and act opens the door to increased self-awareness and self-knowledge. I grew up in a household that valued good grades, thus good grades were programmed into my thought process at an early age. Some programming from childhood is benign or serves us well. On the contrary, others can be harmful or limiting. If you are programmed to think that exercise is bad, that belief could ripple out beyond childhood impacting your health into adulthood.

Much like watching television shows gives us a peek into different lines of work or lifestyles, looking at our programming creates a space to explore and grow. Throughout life, we are susceptible to different ways of thinking and perceiving. Separating ourselves out from what others think or feel in order to connect with our own personal thoughts and feelings gives us insight into our minds and inner consciousness. Meditation offers a tool to guide us through the discovery of what drives and what motivates us in our everyday lives.

When you look at programming in your life, you may not have to look far. Start with your day to day - what do you do out of habit? What have you come to believe is something that you have to do? What messages do you tell yourself day in and day out? Do you feel confined to do/act/feel/think a certain way? Have you been programmed to believe you have to be a certain way to have value?

Not all programming is inherently good or bad. When looking at the rules that govern your life, consider implementing a spectrum or ranking system. For instance, the programming that you aren't good at basketball and should stick with musical instruments may not have been such an issue for you since you didn't really want to play sports. However, now that you are older and your friends have a pick up game each week, you would like to play. Can you let your outdated programming slide away so that you can join the game? While that may seem like a rather trivial example, when programming plays a part in matters tied to financial or relationship success, digging into the rules we have told ourselves or followed becomes paramount to our growth. What are we missing out on if we allow outdated programs to run in the background?

After feeling like we circled the same place every few months in our relationship at one point in our marriage, my spouse and I made the connection that each of our own ingrained programming kept restricting our communication. Our communication programming was impacting our ability to move forward in our relationship. We relived the same cycle we grew up experiencing. It took time, meditation and outside perspectives for us to see it and then unravel it. Understanding the pictures we both had in regards to communication in relationships served as a step toward us developing our own communication style and truths that matched our present time needs. We designed strategies to help each other reprogram our old habits and implement new communication systems. While we are not perfect, our communication has greatly improved.

Meditation is an avenue to explore your own programming. Start by setting your space, grounding, and filling in with your energy. Then look at pictures representing the ways programming impacts your life and how you work within the "rules." Let the pictures offer you insight into who you are, what guides you, and what you might shift in order to navigate areas of your life with more ease. When you are conscious of the programming that guides you, life opens up in a new way. You see more, you experience more, you have a freedom to navigate life with a different sense of knowing.

When I realized all those years ago that following the rules was in my best interest, it created space for me to know myself on a deeper level. When a friend suggested a shortcut on our way home, I knew right away, I would be the one that would get caught, yelled at, lost, in trouble or who knows what. I didn't have to think twice. I could say no thanks without a big explanation. When you know yourself, decisions become easier. While I make it a habit to check in with my programming regularly, this is one that hasn't varied.

Societal rules maintain freedoms and safety for us all. This is an invitation to discover programming for yourself. Looking at your programming and knowing yourself more fully to be true to yourself and what you are here to create, do and have, makes investigating what governs your space and your life a powerful aid in fulfilling what you came here to do.

Before we jump into our meditation looking at programming, I want to touch upon a technique called running energy. It is akin to filling ourselves with our unique energy vibration or adding in neutral gold. When running energy here, I'm referencing the practice of letting energy intentionally flow through meridians in our body. These energy channels are like highways for energy. Energy can flow fast or slow or sometimes get stuck.

The body has energy channels throughout. To run your energy, you will visualize moving Earth energy (energy below the ground) and cosmic energy (energy above the ground) through energy channels in your body. This technique moves energy in the body to ensure energy does not get stuck while in meditation. Let yourself see the channels as they appear to you rather than get too caught up in specifics. Intentions go a long way in meditation and energy work.

This meditation will also reference chakras. Chakras are energetic centers in the body that look like spinning cones lying on their sides. There are seven main chakras lining up from the base of the spine to the crown of the head as well as chakras throughout the body such as in the hands and feet. We will run energy and adjust chakras in this and subsequent meditations.

Meditation: Programming

Programming serves as a safety measure and/or cultural mores. It is key when looking to make changes in your life. The programming you tune in to, consciously or unconsciously, influences how you live and what you allow yourself to undertake. This meditation aims at highlighting how to know when it might be time for a beneficial change or tune-up to your programming. This meditation marks an opportunity to see, to learn and to gain information about the programming you are working and playing with right now. Let's get started!

When you are ready, take a deep breath, and close your eyes.

As you settle into your space, wiggling your toes and fingers, connecting to your body, noticing how you are feeling and doing, move your attention to the center of your head – that space for neutrality and non-judgment – behind your eyes. Give yourself a breath or two as you notice how it feels to be in the center of your head at this moment. When you are ready, create a new grounding cord for this meditation, connecting a cord from the base of your spine to the center of the Earth. The grounding cord can be anything, a tree trunk, a line of color, a rope, whatever looks or feels good at this moment. Then widen out the grounding cord to encompass your entire body and the space that surrounds you. Notice as you ground, you can release and relax, letting your body be supported by this grounding cord. Let this grounding cord create a tunnel or a passageway to release and let go of energy you may be holding onto and no longer serves you. Release it now. Usher it back to where it rightfully belongs.

See your gold sun shining down filling you in with your unique vibration, offering a healing to you. Take a deep breath, pause and notice how you are feeling after releasing unwanted energy and infusing your space with your energy.

Begin to bring Earth energy up through your feet chakras located at the soles of your feet, up your leg channels through your first chakra located at the base of your spine. Then send it back down to the center of the Earth. Keep running this cycle without effort. Next, bring cosmic energy into your body through your crown chakra located at the top of your head down your back channels to your first chakra. Mix the cosmic energy with Earth energy in the first chakra and bring cosmic with a splash of Earth energy up the front channels branching down the arms and out the hands while also going up to the crown chakra to fountain out through the crown chakra. Keep both energies running simultaneously with intention as we continue into our meditation.

With your energy running, see and have your gold sun shining down filling you in with your unique vibration, offering a healing to you. Take a deep breath, pause and notice how you are feeling.

Set a bubble or protection around your space, whatever looks or feels best to you. See a rose or object of your choosing out in front of you and blow it up. Create a few more objects and then blow them up. Remind yourself that you can create and destroy. Give yourself permission as you are creating and destroying out in front of you from your mind's eye to let the process be a healing, a release of energy, and a way to keep things moving so as to not get stuck. If you are feeling stuck, use this space to blow roses with the intention to clear what is causing you or your energy to feel stuck or slowed.

Give yourself a few deep breaths as you settle into your space, notice how you are feeling, and any thoughts that may pop up. As images, ideas, information, colors, pictures and/or feelings come up, take note, have them. Give yourself permission to release them down your grounding cord. If you notice yourself drifting out of meditation, simply pull back to the center of your head. No effort.

During this meditation, we will work with our lower three body chakras turned down and our crown chakra set to gold. We do this to give ourselves space to see the information rather than feel it all on a body level. Continue to keep your energy running (Earth and cosmic energy) in the background in order to keep the body in present time as we move through looking at programming. As you notice, see and receive information and insights, new information may pop up.

To turn down the lower chakras, with intention, set your first chakra to be about 10% open. Very simply from the center of your head, notice your first chakra, located just above the base of your spine, and set it to about 10% open.

Next, tune into your second chakra, located above the first chakra and just below the belly button along the spine. Again, from the center of your head, set your second chakra to be about 10% open.

Lastly, say hello to your third chakra, your solar plexus chakra, and from the center of your head, set your third chakra to about 50% open. Once you have set your chakras, give yourself a few deep breaths and create and destroy a few more roses. With intention, set your crown chakra (your seventh chakra located at the top of your head) to gold.

While gold is a high vibration, it is a lower vibration than white allowing us to be present in our bodies as we see and notice the information coming up during the meditation. Working from the center of our heads, our third eye, allows us to see from neutrality. When we can see something, we can work with it, clear it, move it, have it, or whatever else we need to do. When we see something, we create space to release the old and foster change, for new to come in.

As you give yourself a deep breath and continue to run energy through your energy channels, look out from the center of your head. See the picture or word that pops up for you when you hear the word programming as I have described it. Specifically look at where you have been programmed in your life. One picture may pop up, a few pictures may pop up, you may see pieces of lots of pictures, you may get a sense of different scenarios, or you may see words, or colors. Programming looks different to everyone, as all things do. As you are sitting in meditation, create space to look at programming and what that word conjures up for you.

Give yourself a deep breath and notice what has been popping up for you – thoughts, feelings, images, as you are opening up the space to look at programming.

Let's take a closer look at a few big areas for programming: relationships, career, health, and finances.

Where are you programmed when it comes to relationships? Relationships with a partner, family members, children, friends, co-workers, neighbors? See whatever picture pops up first, noting that you may see things as colors, words, symbols, images, or thoughts – this is simply a chance to sit and notice and be present to view what comes up. Let yourself have the insights that flow to you. Where are you programmed when it comes to relationships? Is the information you are working with relevant to where you are in your life right now?

Blow up a rose. Notice you are in the center of your head. Let information come up and have your neutrality with it. Breathe.

Where are you programmed in regards to your career? Is your picture showing that your career has to unfold a certain way because that is how someone in your life did it? Is there only one correct way to approach your career? Do you set expectations for yourself that don't match what you really want to do or be? Were you given the message growing up that you needed to have a certain job to be successful or valued as a person? How is that programming working or not working for you? Notice what appears to you.

Again, breathe. Pause. Reflect. See for yourself. Let yourself have the information. If you drift out of the center of your head, pull your attention right back behind your eyes, create and destroy a rose or two to get the energy moving in your space, have your energy running and settle back into your meditation..

Where are you programmed in your health? Do you eat certain foods because someone told you that is what you like to eat? Do you avoid foods that you crave because someone told you not to eat them? Is your body communicating with you, yet you are not listening because of programming? Are you participating in health related programming that doesn't actually work for you? Maybe a meal schedule, a workout regime, or a diet plan? Let yourself notice, let yourself see.

Keep breathing. Keep creating and destroying, clearing out energy. You can come back to any of these pictures whenever you want. You can revisit the information popping up and delve deeper. This meditation is about highlighting a few areas of programming.

While still in the center of the head, make space to look at where you are programmed in your finances, your wealth, and your prosper-

ity. Are you programmed to look at your finances from a place of abundance or scarcity? Did you get the message that money is easy to earn and have? Have you programmed yourself to react a certain way to having money? To saving money? To spending money? Take a look. No pressure. No right or wrong. Simply notice and have the information coming up.

Pop a bubble or blow up a rose.

Give yourself a deep breath. Create and destroy a few more objects.

Programming is a big topic. One to notice as you move through your day-to-day life, in meditation and out of meditation. As you continue in meditation, set an intention right now to pay attention to programming on your path. Decide to consciously create your life with programming in mind. As you notice programming, you can change or update the programming instantly. As you clear outdated information or pictures by seeing them and grounding them out, create new pictures to take the place of the old programmed pictures. Set the intention to consciously foster new programming going forward.

Fill in with lots of gold and release anything that came up during the meditation down your grounding cord. As you are releasing, fill in anywhere you have cleared energy or released old information with your gold sun energy – your unique vibration. Have your space be full of your energy. Blow another rose or two. Blow a rose for programming. Blow a rose for programming in your relationships. Blow a rose for programming in your career. Blow a rose for programming in your health. Blow a rose for programming in your finances. Let your chakras go back to whatever you want them to be set at and have your crown set to whatever vibration or color feels or looks good. When you are ready, come out of meditation connecting back to your surroundings and bringing your awareness back to your body.

Meditation Tips and Tricks:

- This meditation led you through a clairvoyant meditation where your focus was on seeing pictures to gain information and insight into what governs your life and whether this is working for you. If not, it is yours to change so it does work, fit and feel good for you.

- Using meditation techniques such as grounding and working with your unique vibration make it easier to clairvoyantly look at pictures to decipher their meaning.

- The meditation basic techniques prepare your space by clearing out energy that doesn't belong to you to more clearly see your pictures and your information.

- Some pieces of the meditation may feel easy to do and look at while others may feel more challenging. That doesn't mean something is wrong. Keep practicing and remember to bring in amusement.

Questions after Meditating:

- Which programming topics felt easy to look at and see?
- What areas would you like to explore more?
- How does programming show up in your life for good or not so good? What are your next steps in this space?

Chapter 10: Agreements

Did you know when you came into this lifetime you agreed to have 2.5 kids, a dog, a cat, a 50-hour a week job and a father- in-law that doesn't really like you? Did you sign up for that? Surely you didn't.

And yet...did you?

Agreements are everywhere. We consciously and unconsciously enter into them all the time. We sign on the dotted line agreeing to pay our mortgage every month, we fill out a credit card application with the understanding that if we don't pay on time, they will charge us penalties and more interest, and we agree to certain societal norms such as using soft voices in the library. Ideally, every time we enter into an agreement, we would know exactly what we were getting ourselves into and we would line up all the terms from the start. Unfortunately, life happens, things transpire and original agreements don't always stand the test of time. They need to be updated, changed, modified, or adjusted in some way, much like our programming.

We change agreements on the physical level all the time. We start a job and two years in, we ask for different responsibilities or a different work schedule. Agreement changed. We buy a house and decide in five years that we need a bigger space; we sell the house and purchase another one. Agreement changed. We get married and three months in decide we made a mistake. We part ways. Agreement changed. Best case, we make a decision and with relative ease, update the agreement and move forward.

Sometimes agreements can be altered or broken seamlessly and effortlessly. Unfortunately, that is not always the case. In the body, feelings get involved, attachments are made, and all too often, there is complication and conflict. Our boss likes the status quo and doesn't want any change. We want to move, and yet, the market isn't in our favor right now. Our partner doesn't want to end the marriage so resists the divorce or on the contrary, wants to marry and we want to stay as partners.

When it comes to agreements on a spirit level, there is a meditation for that. In meditation, you can look at the energy of the agreements you are in; you can see what is working, what needs updating, what has shifted. You can rewrite the agreements while in meditation by seeing what still works and/or what you would like to change. You can imagine what a new agreement would look like and give yourself permission to see the agreement changed, very similar to programming. In creating the picture of the updated or new agreement, you are making space for the agreement in the physical realm to shift. When we have new or more information, we naturally adjust. Our vibration changes when new pictures are presented. The more we see, the more we know. The more we know, the more possibilities unfold.

In meditation, give yourself permission to look at an agreement you want to update. It could be something minor (that your roommate does the dishes more nights a week than you do) or something more complex (an agreement with your twenty nine coworkers that the company moves its headquarters from Omaha to Seattle). In energy, there isn't a hierarchy - energy is energy. Happy and sad are both energies. It's only in the physical that we attach to the notion that happiness is good and sadness is bad. Simple or complex, it is all energy. From your mind's eye, your third eye, the center of your head, see the updated space or agreement you want to have. See that your roommate is doing the dishes. See that the office all moves to Seattle. Let yourself imagine it, rewrite the agreement, see it as a picture, as a contract, however it appears to you.

As you see it in front of you, as you picture it, notice how you feel, what you experience with this new scenario on a body level. If your mind wanders, pull it right back to the center of your head. Any thoughts that pop up, you can send down your grounding cord. You are allowing yourself to work in a space of creating. As you see the agreements you want to adjust, you are not only rewiring your energy, you are shifting how you respond to others. The power of this is in that rewiring. Then, when you actually experience the shift on the physical level, the space already exists in spirit for you to have it. You have cleared a path through clear seeing.

While you can't change others, you can change yourself. Looking at agreements in meditation is not about forcing change upon others. When you let yourself see the possibilities, look at what you want and bring your agreements to present time, you shift your energy. You can adjust. Naturally when you make a shift, others shift too. They may not know they are shifting; yet they are.

Ever started a challenge like eating differently and all of a sudden you notice your partner or best friend eats differently too? Or started reading more and then your family starts reading more too? Growth is contagious. It's one of the reasons we love babies so much - they are constantly growing and changing which gives us permission to grow and change too.

As you update and adjust agreements, everyone around you gets to do the same, consciously or unconsciously. While we often do this unconsciously, it is more powerful when we consciously choose the agreements we want to shift.

My husband and I have kept a marriage journal since we tied the knot four kids, two cities, and one dog ago. We use it to track growth and change over the years and, yes, to keep our agreement in present time. We like to meet every year and check in on our agreement as a couple. We have a set of questions that we both answer and then share the answers to aloud to gain insights with and for each other. We have found it mutually beneficial to actively keep our agreement in present time. While I am optimistic about our future, I do not claim this in any way guarantees happiness and decades of marital bliss. It reminds us to mindfully navigate our individual and collective growth and to see each other, physically, emotionally and spiritually. The check-in has allowed us to shift future goals and bring pieces of our individual pictures together to better support each other.

In a perfect world, agreements would all be amicably negotiated and updated whenever needed. Meditation mitigates the stress and friction you may feel when agreements don't feel like they fit anymore.

As you look to grow and change, review your agreements. What governs you? What is lining up that you have agreed to and what needs to change? As pictures pop up in meditation, update the agreements as you see them. See it in spirit and then let the space you create in meditation translate to the physical too. When you shift from spirit, the effects ripple down to the mind and body. Use the techniques you have practiced in meditation to see and update agreements. You are powerful at manifesting and creating beyond the physical limitations of the body. Let yourself create space for moving past outdated agreements and onto your next steps.

Meditation: Agreements

Agreements are everywhere. From the small agreements that are short and sweet to bigger agreements – the sign on the dotted line agreements, the binding agreements and the forever agreements. There is a lot happening!

Every so often, pausing to take stock of the agreements you are working with, to bring agreements into present time, to let go of past agreements that no longer serve a purpose and to consciously move into new agreements proves helpful in navigating what you are creating in your life. We will use this meditation to look at our agreements, bring our awareness to the agreements we create and consciously notice we can shift agreements we are ready to move out of or end.

So let's dive in and take a look!

When you are ready, take a deep breath and close your eyes.

As you settle into your space, wiggling your toes and fingers, connecting to your body, noticing how you are feeling and doing, move your attention to the center of your head – that space for neutrality and non-judgment. Give yourself a breath or two as you notice how it feels to be in the center of your head at this moment. When you are ready, create a new grounding cord for this meditation, connecting a cord from your first chakra to the center of the Earth. The grounding cord can be anything, a tree trunk, a line of color, a roller coaster track, whatever looks or feels good in this moment. Then widen out the grounding cord to encompass your entire body and aura, the space that surrounds you. Notice as you are grounded, you can release and relax, letting your body be supported by this grounding cord. Let this grounding cord create a tunnel or a passageway to release and let go of energy you may be holding onto and are ready to release.

Begin to bring Earth energy up through your feet chakras, up your leg channels through your first chakra and back down to the center of the Earth and then bring cosmic energy down through your crown chakra down the back channels, mixing with a little Earth energy in the first and coming back up the front channels branching down the arms and out the hands while also fountaining out through the crown chakra.

With your energy running, see and have your energy shining down filling you in with your unique vibration, offering a healing to you. Take a deep breath, pause and notice how you are feeling.

Set a bubble or protection around your space. Then see a bubble or object out in front of you and blow it up. Create and destroy a few times - picking an object or a bubble and blowing it up, popping it, dissolving it or evaporating it. Remind yourself that you can create and destroy. Give yourself permission as you are creating and destroying to let the process be a healing, a release and letting go of energy. This is a way to keep things moving so as to not get stuck. If you are feeling stuck, use this space to look at a picture of what might be behind the stuck energy. Then notice you can put that energy out in front of you and ground it out, see it blow up or dissolve, and fill back in with your energy.

Take a few deep breaths as you settle into your space, notice how you are feeling, and the thoughts that may pop up. As images, information, colors, pictures or feelings arise, take note, have it, and then release it or blow it up. If you notice yourself drifting out of meditation, no problem, simply pull back to the center of your head. No effort.

During this meditation, we will work with our lower three body chakras turned down and our crown chakra set to gold. We do this to help ourselves stay in the center of our head, the space for neutrality, and to give ourselves space to see the information rather than feel it all on a body level. We will continue to keep our energy running lightly (Earth and cosmic energy) in order to keep the body in present time as we move through looking at agreements. As you notice, see, and receive information and insights, new things may pop up or you may be reminded of past information.

This meditation is an opportunity to see, to learn and to gain information about the agreements you are working and playing with right now.

To turn down the lower chakras, set your first chakra to be about 10-15% open. Very simply from the center of your head, notice your first chakra, located just above the base of your spine, and set it to about 10% open.

Next, tune into your second chakra, located just a little bit above the first chakra, below the belly button along the spine. Again, from the center of your head, set your second chakra to be about 10% open.

Lastly, say hello to your third chakra, your solar plexus chakra, and also from the center of your head, set your third chakra to about 50% open.

Once you have set your chakras, give yourself a few deep breaths and create and destroy a few more images or pop a few more bubbles. Notice that creating and destroying is a way to keep energy moving during a meditation. Then, again with intention, set your crown chakra (your seventh chakra located at the top of your head) to gold.

While gold is a high vibration, it is a lower vibration than white allowing us to be present in our bodies as we see and notice the information coming up during the meditation. Working from the center of our heads, our third eye, allows us to see from neutrality. When we can see something, we can work with it, clear it, move it, have it, or whatever else we need to do. When we see something, we open the door to understanding and solving it.

Tapping into your ability to see and know your own answers is powerful. When you know your truth, life takes on a new meaning as you move through your days having your answers. It lends itself to clarity.

As you continue to settle into your space, into the center of your head, your lower three chakras turned down, your crown chakra set at gold, your energy running lightly, gold sun filling in your space, protection roses or a bubble around you giving you a space to be, notice you can create another image or two and blow them up.

From the center of your head, take a look at a picture of agreements – what pops up for you when you think of or look at agreements? Does a person come up? What image, word or visual pops up when you hear the word agreements? Perhaps you see pictures of lots of different agreements, small agreements, or perhaps a bigger agreement comes into view.

Maybe you are negotiating with an employer for a new job position and the agreement isn't settled yet, maybe you are working on a new proposal for a client, maybe you are purchasing a property. Those agreements are often easier to look at and see at first as they physically require us to sign something stating we agree to the terms – we agree to pay X amount for a house, we agree to do this project - making them obvious agreements.

Notice as you are sitting in this space if other agreements surface. Agreements you may not readily think about. Agreements with siblings as to birth order for example – might you have had an agreement with a brother or a sister that he or she goes first or second? Agreements are formed every day in the body and the spirit. In the body, we work with the agreements, re-negotiating them, sometimes to the point of frustration. The power of looking and seeing them in meditation is that we can set the space differently – we see the information and then more easily change it on a body level.

Continue to notice what is popping up for you.

Meditation creates the space to see your answers and move forward.

As you are looking at agreements appearing for you, see how many agreements you are working with right now. See what number pops up. It may surprise you.

Continue to breathe. Using the technique of creating and destroying as you move through the meditation to continue to clear energy as you look at agreements in your space.

As you see agreements, you can ground them, run neutral gold through them, you can re-write them, and even blow them up – use the power of visualization to create space in the body to move forward in your life with ease and grace, less effort. When you see something, you can clear it or create it.

Pop a bubble.

Focus on you. What agreement do you have with yourself, with your body, with your mind, with your spirit? Are you in alignment with the agreement you have with you? What is the agreement you have with your body? Are you looking to be a marathoner, when in this lifetime running doesn't work for you? Are you pushing your body, mind and spirit without updating the agreement? Are you asking yourself for something either it's not time for or your body isn't in alignment with?

We all know when you attempt to make an agreement with someone that doesn't want to be in agreement with you, it doesn't usually work out well. You meet resistance. Are you or your body resisting something you have been attempting to do? Give yourself space to see it now. On the flip side, if you are seeing agreements and they are working for you then you are in alignment with them. Run gold through them and ground them. Reinforce the pictures.

Agreements can change. We can enter an agreement planning one thing and then things change. If you fail to communicate that, the things you wanted to change about the plan most likely won't happen. The same is true for the agreements we have with ourselves. We may have made an agreement with ourselves when growing up and it no longer works. We may have asked our bodies to do different things and as we aged, things shifted and changed, yet did we update the agreement? Take a moment to update or verify the agreements you have with you. Let the body know. Communicate the new picture of what you are creating to your body by telling yourself the new information or showing yourself a picture. Remember, we think in pictures. Paint a new picture out in front of your mind's eye and program that picture in as your updated agreement.

If you want to change the agreement you have with yourself, create a new picture for your body, mind, and spirit. See what you want to manifest or change. Create a visual – in your mind's eye – see yourself as you would like to be in present time. Bring your agreement with yourself to present time by seeing a new picture. Notice the details. See for yourself and give yourself permission to release an old or outdated agreement or bring in a new or updated agreement or picture. You can modify, edit, or change the picture or agreement to meet your needs and wants now. Go for it! We work best in pictures. Visualize the picture, the agreement, of you, as you want to be!

Pop a few bubbles or blow a few roses. Put the agreement or agreements you were looking at with yourself in a rose and blow it up. Give yourself a few deep breaths and see or feel that you are still grounded and connected to the center of the Earth. Take a moment to fill in with your gold sun everywhere you may have just released or cleared energy from your space.

Next, notice the agreements you have with other people in your life. What agreement or agreements are you in with other people in your life? Focus on one or two during this meditation, and see what pops up. It may be a person or picture of you doing something with someone. You may have an agreement with your job or your partner. You may have an agreement with a child or a friend. See the agreement and ask yourself if it is working for you. What is the agreement about? Are you still in alignment with the agreement?

If you are in agreement with the picture, use neutral gold and see or visualize that neutral gold running through the picture, giving the agreement a healing, clearing off other people's energy on the agreement that doesn't need to be there.

As we work together and move through life with people, other people's pictures and energy invades our space. We take on other people's ideas, thoughts, and feelings – not on purpose. As you are looking at the agreement that appeared or popped up, see that you can clear other people's information off the agreement in order to have it more cleanly for yourself.

If the agreement you are looking at is not working for you, intuit what you need to do to bring the agreement into present time to work for you once again. To clear other people out of an agreement, run neutral gold through an agreement. Gold works as a healing on the agreement to clear off other people's energy, like windshield wipers clearing away raindrops.

Another option, if the agreement you are looking at is no longer a fit, is old or outdated, let it go by grounding it out or put it in a rose or object of your choosing and blow it up. Re-create a new agreement in its place. Notice this may involve two steps. First, see or create a new agreement in meditation. Then, on a physical level, take the information seen with you to communicate or set up a new agreement with the person. When you see an agreement that no longer is working, healing it or clearing it in meditation helps pave the way in the body. Use meditation to set the tone to bring updated or new information into the body.

As agreements appear in meditation, validate that things shift and change. You change, the individuals you were or are in agreement with change. Consciously recognizing that creates space to update the agreements and see people where they are now.

Create and destroy an object or poop a bubble for the agreement you were studying. At any time you can look at an agreement. See the pic-

ture of it from neutrality. Look for yourself at what makes sense, what is needed, what is working or not working.

Working the agreement on a spirit level in meditation helps ease transitions on a body level. The more consciousness and awareness you bring to the agreements you are working with, the easier to change, up-date, and modify the agreement. Remember to have amusement with it. Keep it light. See, learn, and gain clarity about how you want to be and move forward in relation to agreements in your life.

Blow a picture or pop a bubble. Give yourself a deep breath. Create and destroy a few more times. Fill in with lots of gold and release any-thing that came up during the meditation down your grounding cord. As you release, fill in anywhere you have cleared energy or old infor-mation with your gold sun energy - your unique vibration. Have your space be full of your energy. Pop a bubble for agreements. Let your chakras go back to whatever you want them to be set at and have your crown set to whatever vibration or color feels or looks good. When you are ready, come out of meditation, bringing your attention back to your body.

Meditation Tips and Tricks:

- Exploring agreements is a way to gain insight and bring clarity into your life.
- Agreements are made consciously and unconsciously, in the physical world and also in the spiritual realm.
- Looking at agreements opens the door to movement and growth.
- Agreements, as with spirit in general, are sometimes easier to clear or modify on a spirit level than on a body level. Since we have a body, we need to bring the new or updated information into the body in order to take the next steps in our life.

Questions after Meditating:

- Did certain agreements instantly appear in your meditation? Are there others you sense exist but couldn't see this time?
- Was it easier to see agreements with yourself or with others?
- When looking at agreements, how did your physical body feel? Did anything come up that created discomfort?
- Did you find yourself wanting to analyze the agreements as opposed to looking at them from neutrality?

Chapter 11: Limitations

When you are two years old, limitations for how far you can wander off from your caretaker or what you can do on your own make sense. When you are forty-two and still heavily limiting yourself on where and what you can do and create in your life, it might indicate a problem.

What would you do, be or have if there was nothing to limit you? Not even if the sky was the limit? Can you imagine the possibilities for yourself?

Limitations can serve as a comfort and a way to stay in our safe zones. When we let go of limitations, we may not know what we are releasing. Limitations can be self imposed or placed upon us by others. We can line up with the limitations other people put on themselves as well. Our best friend works a certain job and in order to stay friends, we take the same or similar job. We could be the manager, however, we don't want to invalidate our friend, so we stay where we are at an entry level. We limit our growth potential. People tell us over and over again all that we could do and have more. Yet, we stay where we are for the sake of the friendship and we get used to the routine in our lives.

The intention behind a person's actions may not be to control or limit. Your friend most likely wasn't consciously asking you to stay in the same job to be like them. Sometimes it is with the best of intentions that people in our lives limit us. They may have set limitations as a protection and then not looked back to see if those limits were still applicable. When you were a child, a parent may have limited you to playing in the backyard, as you got older, ideally the parent let you have more freedom. Sometimes we change faster than the pictures others have of us. The picture may limit us when that was not the original intent simply because the picture is outdated or not in present time. When you can see the picture, it opens up space for healing and moving past the limitation. You can run gold through the picture, release it down your grounding cord, or blow it up from your mind's eye. Clearing the picture in meditation makes it easier to move past the picture on the physical plain.

Growing up, I moved around a fair amount. As I looked back, I realized what a gift moving was for my growth. I wasn't limited by who I was at 5 years old because no one knew me from back then. My 15 year old self wasn't limited to what my 10 year old self wanted to be because all anyone saw was who I was in the present moment. The moves worked for me as it allowed me to explore and recreate myself anew without limits. I ended up playing ice hockey for a short period of time, something I never would have done if we had stayed in the small town I lived in prior to moving. Though at the time, moving did not seem like a win. It felt limiting, like punishment, not as healing or helpful to my overall growth, despite my parents framing it as an opportunity for us all.

Limitations take many forms and even false representations. Giving yourself a chance to look and see what is limiting you creates an opportunity for healing. As you navigate your life looking for limitations or pictures of possible limitations, you may see people, events and situations from an entirely different vantage point. As your perspective shifts, your awareness increases; you gain information that allows you to grow in ways you never thought possible. To explore and look at pictures of the energy of limitations (real or perceived) present in your life, you gain insights and awareness.

Perhaps the goal is complete limitlessness. Perhaps the goal is merely a better understanding of your own limitations. Perhaps the goal is clearing out other people's limitations from your space. Regardless of the goal, the discoveries made from looking at this concept will forever shift your experience of your life and all that follows. You get to decide. Your former limits can set you free to have the journey you most desire.

Meditation: Limitations

It has been said that the only limitations are the ones you put on yourself. We are going to take it one step further to see and acknowledge the limitations by also looking at what may be acting as a barrier to limit forward momentum in your life. By acknowledging the pictures and information, we go beyond to discover more about ourselves and reach new heights.

Let's get started!

When you are ready, sit with your feet on the floor, give yourself a deep breath, and close your eyes. As you settle into your space, connect to your body, noticing how you are feeling and doing, move your attention to the center of your head – that space for neutrality and not judgment – behind your eyes. Give yourself a breath or two as you notice how it feels to be in the center of your head at this moment. When you are ready, give yourself a new grounding cord for this meditation, connecting a cord from your first chakra to the center of the Earth. The grounding cord can be anything, a tree trunk, a line of color, a rope, whatever looks or feels good in this moment. Widen out the grounding cord to encompass your entire body and aura, the space that surrounds you. Notice as you are grounded, you can release and relax, letting your body be supported by this grounding cord. Let this grounding cord create a tunnel or a passageway to release and let go of energy you may be holding onto and are ready to release.

Begin to bring Earth energy up through your feet chakras, up your leg channels through your first chakra and back down to the center of the Earth. Then bring cosmic energy down through your crown chakra down the back channels, mixing with a little Earth energy in the first and coming back up the front channels branching down the arms and out the hands and fountaining out through the crown chakra.

With your energy running, see and have your gold sun shining down filling you in with your unique vibration, offering a healing to you. Take a deep breath, pause and notice how you are feeling.

Set a bubble or other protection around your space, however it looks or feels best to you. And then pop a few bubbles or create and destroy as you have practiced. Remind yourself that you can create and destroy. Give yourself permission as you are creating and destroying out in front of you from your mind's eye to let the process of releasing energy be a healing, a letting go of energy, and a way to keep things moving so as to not get stuck. If you feel stuck, go ahead and use this space to blow some roses with the intention to clear what is making you feel that way.

Take a few deep breaths as you settle into your space, notice how you are feeling, and the thoughts that may pop up. As things, images, information, colors, pictures or feelings come up, take note, have it and give yourself permission to release it.

Acknowledging what you are seeing or noticing gives the picture or information space to be seen, to be understood, to be processed. It's in seeing it, recognizing it and owning it that we can move forward, change and grow.

If you notice yourself drifting out of the center of your head, no problem, simply pull back to the center of your head. No effort.

During this meditation, we will work with our lower three body chakras turned down and our crown chakra set to gold. Turning down the chakras helps us to stay in the center of our head, the space for neutrality, and to give ourselves room to see the information rather than feel it all on a body level. We will continue to keep our energy running (Earth and cosmic energy) in the background in order to keep the body in present time as we move through looking at limitations.

As you notice, see and receive information and insights, be conscious that you don't have to do anything about the information, simply having the information is enough during the meditation. Action comes later. Give yourself space in this meditation, gather the information and after your meditation you can bring it into the body to process and act on the information. Meditation creates the space to get a clear picture of what actions to take on a body level post-meditation.

When you have a clear picture of what's happening or what needs to happen, it is much easier to make it real and tangible. Use this meditation as an opportunity to see the limits, where you might be handling controls or pictures limiting your next steps, and then take the information out into your life to move forward.

To turn down the lower chakras, set your first chakra to be about 10% open. From the center of your head, notice your first chakra, located just above the base of your spine, and set it to about 10% open.

Next, tune into your second chakra, located a little bit above the first chakra, below the belly button along the spine. From the center of your head, set your second chakra to be about 10% open.

Lastly, say hello to your third chakra, your solar plexus chakra, and also from the center of your head, set your third chakra to about 50% open.

Once you have set your chakras, give yourself a few deep breaths and create and destroy a few more roses. With intention, set your crown chakra (your seventh chakra located at the top of your head) to gold.

While gold is a high vibration, it is a lower vibration than white allowing us to be present in our bodies as we see and notice the information coming up during the meditation. Working from the center of our heads, our third eye, allows us to see from neutrality.

As we release energy or information in our space that no longer serves us or is not our true vibration, we give ourselves more space to have our truth. When we stand in our truth, often we experience life with less effort. When we do not feel limited to explore, grow and do what is in our highest and best, we can move forward and discover more of ourselves in the process.

Limitations are everywhere. As you continue to settle into your space, notice what you are seeing and what is popping up in your space.

What do limitations look like to you? When you think of limitations, does something or someone pop up? Do you feel limited by someone or something in your life?

It is not challenging to find someone that will tell you something about what you are doing being wrong or invalid. People love to share their thoughts and opinions. When you run into someone that says something that might create doubt or uncertainty, while they may have not done it on purpose, they may have inadvertently created a limiting picture for you – a picture or a thought in your space that causes you to feel uncertain about what you are doing.

Ask yourself what are your next steps with the picture of limitation you are seeing. Notice what pops up when you ask. See for yourself how to move from meditation into action in order to advance in what you want to do or have in your life.

Breathe as you create and destroy images popping up. See the information and release the picture. Have your energy running gently in the background as you notice the pictures, the feelings and the thoughts popping up.

Next, take a look at what may be limiting you from taking your next step, whatever that step may be. Is anything limiting you from standing in your truth and power? Are you limiting yourself and the next step you want to take? What would help you move to the next level? Are you unconsciously limiting your next steps out of fear or uncertainty or not feeling like you know you should?

Take a look and ask. What information do you need to move forward? What would be helpful to know right now as you continue to create and manifest whatever you most want to have in your life? Connect, right now, to your truth and your information. See for yourself your next step.

Validate everything you see or notice – even if it doesn't make sense right now. Trust that whatever is popping up is for a reason and you don't need to know that reason right now. Allow yourself to see. Notice what you are feeling. Sit in your space. From the center of your head, notice what you need to move forward – it could be a thought, a picture, a color, a shape, a symbol – the information can come in many forms. Be present to see.

Keep creating and destroying, moving the energy. Noticing what you are seeing for your next steps as you have said hello to the energy of limitation in your space. Remember to be gentle on yourself as you highlight this information and see your next steps.

Continue to breathe. Fill in with lots of gold and when you are ready destroy or release the pictures that appeared.

Fill in with lots of gold and release anything that came up during the meditation down your grounding cord. As you are releasing, fill in anywhere you have cleared energy or released old information with your gold sun energy – your unique vibration. Have your space be full of your energy. Create an image for limitations and then destroy it. Let your chakras go back to whatever you want them to be set at and have your crown set to whatever vibration or color feels or looks good. When you are ready, come out of meditation, take a deep breath and come back to your body.

Meditations Tips and Tricks:

- Even if a picture doesn't make sense at the moment, let yourself see it and sit with it. As energy changes, you may begin to understand the picture more.
- Reading pictures gets easier and easier as you practice. You may develop a short-hand language for yourself when you see a color, symbol, shape or picture, and it instantly means something to you.
- This and the other meditations are designed to be revisited as your meditation and clairvoyance grows. Return to these meditations to see what else arises for you whenever you'd like.

Questions after Meditating:

- What limitations felt empowering to see? Did any serve you well? Were there any you released?
- As you released any limitations, did you notice a shift in your physical body?

Chapter 12: Certainty

The difference between beginners and me when it comes to reading energy is simple: certainty. I have spent a lot of my time seeing, looking at and reading energy. We all have something we feel confident and comfortable in performing or have complete certainty about. Maybe it's making pancakes, caring for your elderly mother, changing a tire or making an audience laugh. We have something we either are natural at or have practiced long and hard to master. When you work from certainty, whatever you are doing instantly becomes easier. Have you ever noticed that?

When my husband and I first got married, we adopted a dog. I had never owned a dog growing up nor had my husband. I was out of my element. My husband took to training our dog rather quickly. He had a confidence and command that I didn't initially know I possessed too. Even though he really had no more knowledge than I did about training, he did it in such a way that both the dog and I believed him. He said, "sit," she sat. When I uttered, "sit," the dog looked at me confused as to whether I wanted her to sit or come give me a hug. What was the difference between my husband and me? Certainty. He had it, I didn't.

When it came to babies, I had certainty in spades. In addition, the souls that joined our family unit had their certainty. They didn't stop to question if they should cry now because they were hungry, they just cried. They didn't question if they should wait to have a cookie in a little bit, they wanted a cookie in that moment. The certainty that children have reminds us to have more of it ourselves. When a child wants to play with someone on the playground, they go over to them and start playing. When we find someone we like, we may skirt around it, hint at liking to go out with them and hope that they ask us instead of sticking our neck out first. While there is something to be said for the patience to wait and see, a bit of certainty goes a long way in clearing up miscommunications and misunderstandings swiftly so we don't waste time and energy.

People that have mastered authentic certainty, they aren't playing a part, rather being their true selves, attract people with relative ease. The secret is that they have practiced trusting themselves to know they can handle what unfolds. They have certainty in themselves to show up and navigate what follows. Yes, there are those that pretend or put on airs, in the end, those who authentically show up and own who they are with certainty are revealed.

Certainty is like any other energy. If you want it, bring it into your space. If you want to be happy, do more things that make you happy. If you want more sleep, go to bed earlier. If you want to experience more certainty, do more things that you feel confident about until it is an energy you understand and can easily move in and out of regardless of the situation.

A yogi will say that if you can't get to the mat to practice yoga, do the practice in your mind's eye. Same thing applies here. Not sure where your certainty lies? In meditation, ask for pictures of you having your certainty. See yourself doing what you feel confident doing or what you want to gain confidence in doing. Notice how it feels, whom you are with, where you are and what surrounds you. Then create it in the physical body. Bring those elements into your space in real time. If you were wearing purple in your picture, wear your favorite purple shirt more often. If you were out with friends, invite your friends out. Pave the way to experiencing the energy you would like to have through seeing it from your mind's eye first.

This works with any energy. If you would like to experience more joy, as you settle into your meditation, look for pictures of you experiencing joy. Ask questions as you see what pops up in front of your mind's eye. See yourself having joy. Look at your face, your expression, the colors, the symbols, the places, and the people. If you would like to experience wealth, abundance, health, more friends, a romantic relationship, see it from your mind's eye and note all that the picture has to offer. Let yourself see it. Let yourself envision it. As you do this, you are consciously creating the space for what you want to experience to come into being in your life.

Seeing and reading energy is that simple. It's giving yourself permission to look and see, from the neutral place in the center of your head, no judgment on what appears. As you practice more and more, your certainty with what you see and what you manifest grows. You will become proficient in reading the energy of situations, in understanding what you want, what you need, and how you are feeling. You will know yourself through the pictures you see and the language you have developed to read and interpret what pops up for you in meditation. You will get faster and faster at seeing and knowing. This is all within you, right now. You only need to call it forth.

Meditation: Certainty

Certainty, validation, and amusement are three key elements to creating and having the life you want. When you work with these energies life can feel easier and more fun! Let's get started creating space for certainty, validation, and amusement.

When you are ready, take a deep breath, and close your eyes.

As you settle into your space, wiggling your toes and fingers, connecting to your body, noticing how you are feeling and doing, move your attention to the center of your head – that space for neutrality and not judgment. Give yourself a breath or two as you notice how it feels to be in the center of your head at this moment. When you are ready, give yourself a new grounding cord for this meditation, connecting a cord from your first chakra to the center of the Earth. The grounding cord can be anything, a tree trunk, a line of color, a rope, whatever looks or feels good in this moment. Then widen out the grounding cord to encompass your entire body and the space that surrounds you. Notice as you are grounded, you can release and relax, letting your body be supported by this grounding cord. Let this grounding cord create a tunnel or a passageway to release and let go of energy you may be holding onto and are ready to release.

Begin to bring Earth energy up through your feet chakras, up your leg channels through your first chakra and back down to the center of the Earth and then bring cosmic energy down through your crown chakra down the back channels, mixing with a little Earth energy in the first and coming back up the front channels branching down the arms and out the hands and fountaining out through the crown chakra.

With your energy running, see and have your gold sun shining down filling you in with your unique vibration, offering a healing to you. Take a deep breath, pause and notice how you are feeling.

Set a bubble around your space or protection roses, whichever looks or feels best to you. Then see a rose out in front of you and blow it up. Create a few more roses and then blow them up. Notice you can create and destroy. Give yourself permission as you are creating and destroying roses out in front of you from your mind's eye to let the process of blowing roses be a healing, a release and letting go of energy, and a way to keep things moving so as to not get stuck. If you are feeling stuck, go ahead and use this space to blow some roses with the intention to clear what is making you feel stuck.

Give yourself a few deep breaths as you settle into your space, notice how you are feeling, and the thoughts that may pop up. As things, images, information, colors, pictures, or feelings come up, take note, have it, and give yourself permission to release it or put it in a rose and blow it up. If you notice yourself drifting out of meditation, no problem, simply pull back to the center of your head. No effort.

During this meditation, we will work with our lower three body chakras turned down and our crown chakra set to gold. We do this to help ourselves stay in the center of our head, the space for neutrality, and to give ourselves space to see the information rather than feel it all on a body level. We will continue to keep our energy running (Earth and cosmic energy) in the background in order to keep the body in present time as we move through looking at certainty, validation, and amusement. As you notice, see, and receive information and insights, something may surprise you and other things may not surprise you. There is no right or wrong, simply an opportunity to learn and grow.

Set your first chakra to be about 10% open. Very simply from the center of your head, notice your first chakra, located just above the base of your spine, and set it to about 10% open.

Next, tune into your second chakra, located just a little bit above the first chakra, below the belly button along the spine. Again, from the center of your head, set your second chakra to be about 10% open.

Lastly, say hello to your third chakra, your solar plexus chakra, and also from the center of your head, set your third chakra to about 50% open.

Once you have set your chakras, give yourself a few deep breaths and create and destroy a few more roses. Then, with intention, set your crown chakra (your seventh chakra located at the top of your head) to gold.

While gold is a high vibration, it is a lower vibration than white allowing us to be present in our bodies as we see and notice the information coming up during the meditation. Working from the center of our heads, our third eye, allows us to see from neutrality. When we can see something, we can work with it, clear it, move it, have it, or whatever else we need to do. If we don't see something, don't know something, we can't clear it or solve it. That is the power of seeing and being able to sit in the center of your head and look at your information.

As you continue to settle into your space, into the center of your head, your lower three chakras turned down, your crown chakra set at gold, your energy running lightly, gold sun filling in your space, protection roses or bubble up giving you a space to be, notice you can create another rose or two and blow them up.

In this meditation, we will focus on certainty, validation, and amusement – three major elements in having your space. When tapping into your truth and your ability to see your answers clearly, having certainty, validation, and amusement makes things flow.

As you sit in the center of your head, take a look at certainty. What comes up when you hear the word? Ask yourself, where am I certain? Where do I have certainty? Notice what image, color, word, picture, or thought pops into your space. It can be anything. There is no right or wrong.

Certainty is not about being right all the time. Certainty is about having confidence, having your information and trusting yourself to know for yourself. When you work with certainty, when you move with certainty, the Universe responds and paths open up for you. When you trust yourself and your information, you operate differently than you do or would with doubt or uncertainty. Tuning into your certainty does not mean you will never have another doubt again or that you will never be wrong again; rather it creates space for those things to happen and not be such big deals. You can make a mistake and know that it doesn't have to be a deal breaker – it can happen and pass, you can re-connect to your certainty and move on.

Continue breathing as you notice what images, colors, words or shapes pop up. Then put the picture into a rose and blow it up. Let it go down your grounding cord and clear the picture from your space.

Next, take a look at a picture of when you had certainty. What did that look like? What did that feel like? It can be a simple picture of doing something at work or hanging out with friends. Simply notice what pops up. No right or wrong.

Then put that picture into a rose and blow it up. As you clear out the images or pictures that popped up, notice you can consciously choose to bring more certainty into your space. Right here. Right now. Once you have seen something, you have that information to call upon again.

Next notice validation – what pops up when you hear the word – validation? Are you validated? Do you validate yourself and all you are doing and creating?

Often we seek validation from others – we look to people in our lives to give us feedback that we are doing a good job, we are on the right track, we are okay. When you can find that validation for yourself, life changes.

Take a look now at a picture of what validation looks like to you? How does it feel? Where do you most often feel validated?

Again, continue breathing – noticing what is popping up, seeing the information, hearing the information, however it is popping up for you.

Continue noticing what is popping up, blowing pictures as you go. Staying present, if you drift out, create and destroy and come back to the center of your head, check your grounding, fill in with gold and be right back in the meditation.

As you notice the pictures and information popping up, sprinkle validation into your space. Imagine a big salt shake of validation and sprinkle it into your body and space. You may see it as a certain color, or a certain vibration. Again, no right or wrong. See it for what it looks like to you.

Create and destroy a few roses, continuing to clear the space and keep the energy moving as you blow roses.

I want you to notice what pops up when you hear the word amusement. How often do you play and work with amusement? Are you often amused? Or do you take things seriously? How's that working for you? What comes up for you as you let yourself explore amusement? Take a look at a picture of when you have felt amused – by life, by events, by someone in particular. Keep in mind that amusement does not mean everything is funny. Amusement is the energy of light heartedness and is about keeping things uptempo and not so serious. When was the last time you were amused? See that picture and notice what comes up for you. Notice the colors and the energy of the picture. What does amusement look like to you?

If you are not sure, create and destroy roses, objects, colors or symbols, and let yourself have time and space to allow your information to appear.

Continue breathing and grounding.

Notice, with amusement, are things easier or harder? Take a look at a picture or a time when you were not amused. How did that go? Simply see what pops up, see a picture, and notice what you are feeling.

Amusement helps energy move. When things are serious, they tend to move slowly and with heaviness. When things are filled with amusement, there is a flow and lightness.

Create and destroy roses as you see different pictures.

As you continue to notice and breathe, see what is coming up for you, allow yourself to receive the insights and information. Notice what pictures and information are popping up.

Take a deep breath. Blow another rose or two. Notice certainty, validation, and amusement. Three energies.

Let's tune in to your color for each:

Certainty. See what color pops up for you when you hear the word certainty. Put that color in a rose and blow it up.

Validation. See what color pops up when you hear the word validation. Put that color in a rose and blow it up.

Amusement. See what color pops up when you hear the word amusement. Put that color in a rose and blow it up.

Now you have three colors for three different energies. Use those colors as a healing and as a reminder. If you are out and about and your validation color pops up, be validated. Take it as a reminder to bring validation into your space by filling your space with the color that popped up.

Play with these colors. Let them be part of your daily life. Bring them into the spaces you live and work in most. Use the colors to add amusement and remind yourself to play.

Take a moment to swirl the three colors in and around your space so that you can have your certainty, validation, and amusement. Notice you can come back to these energies and have them in your space anytime and anywhere.

Take a deep breath. Create and destroy. Let your chakras go back to whatever you want them to be and your crown to whatever vibration or color it wants to be. Blow an object or rose that represents certainty, one for validation and one for amusement. When you are ready, come out of meditation.

Meditation Tips and Tricks:

- Finding your certainty is no different than finding your joy or happiness.

- As you work with certainty in meditation, take your practice with you into the world and begin to notice where you observe certainty in yourself and others.

- Validation and amusement are powerful energies to bring into your everyday life.
- Play with colors and use meditation to discover what different colors mean to you.

Questions after Meditating:

- Was it easy to see and work with colors?
- Which energy was easiest to access - certainty, validation, or amusement?
- Are there areas in your life where bringing in the energies of certainty, validation, and amusement could serve you? If so, what areas or places in your life are they?

Chapter 13: Next Steps

If I made a t-shirt, it would say "Danger: Expectations Ahead."

Expectations will get you every time. You go to the store expecting to purchase one thing and walk out with a cart full. You think this is the job for you and two weeks later you learn someone else received the offer instead. You expect a project to go so smoothly and that you will have time to spare. Then it takes double the time and effort predicted or available to you.

You may not even realize you have expectations. You didn't know you were hoping your best friend would bring you a chocolate cake when she showed up with a vanilla one. You didn't know you wanted to have a boy first when you found out it was a girl. You didn't consciously realize that you wanted so badly to get into the same school that your parent/sibling/best friend/neighbor/uncle/third cousin removed went to until you received the rejection letter. Expectations can cause hurt and pain seemingly out of nowhere.

Expectations, when managed, when conscious, set a goal or a picture of what we want to manifest. Think of the self-fulfilling prophecy: expect the best, get the best. When we gear up for success, it puts us in a winning mindset and creates space for optimum outcomes. Why would we approach life any other way? I certainly don't want to order a cake for my birthday expecting it not to turn out to be the most delicious cake I have ever tasted. And yet, when we don't realize our expectations, as the t-shirt says, danger waits.

Not consciously understanding our expectations can set us up for feelings of disappointment, failure, blaming others and the desire to give up. Arguments, disagreements, and break ups result from misunderstood expectations.

Looking at expectations is another avenue of self-discovery. To know what you want from a situation, a person, or an event can prove not only insightful, it serves as another way to manage fallout. If you know there is a cliff ahead, you probably aren't going to run as fast as you are able up to the edge.

Expectations are especially dangerous when we place them on other people. We cannot control how others think, feel or respond. We can only control those aspects for ourselves. When we expect someone to do or react a certain way to something we do or say, we set ourselves up for disappointment. Can you create a space for someone to have the experience they need or want without expecting anything from them?

Parents fall in the expectation trap often. We want our children to be happy when we buy them a new bike, skateboard, trampoline, rollerblades, iPad, and/or puppy. Yet, we don't actually get to decide how they feel about what we gave them. It is the job of the parent to make a decision to the best of their ability and then sit back and allow their child to have the experience they want, need or create.

The key in managing expectations, and one I practice daily, is detachment. The goal is to engage while also mindfully detaching from the outcome. When I get into trouble, I realize it is because I had expectations that I wasn't conscious of having. I attached to an outcome. When I signed my child up for gymnastics, I expected they would love it and would appreciate it so much that when it was time to go to gymnastics, there would be no yelling, resisting or fighting. I unconsciously held expectations and attachments instead of preparing myself for the reality that my child might act any way she might feel in the moment. I had attached to my pictures rather than giving space for her to have her pictures to create the experience she wanted.

I fell for the biggest disappointment involving unconscious expectations when I told my now husband I loved him for the first time. I had a dream that I hadn't told him I loved him and he needed to know. When I woke up, the first words I said were "I love you." His response "I think you are special." To this day, we laugh about it, and yet at that moment, it didn't feel so funny. I unconsciously expected him to declare his mutual affinity for me immediately in response. When he didn't, I felt hurt and invalidated.

Understanding and knowing your expectations beforehand has a profound influence on how you operate in the world. When you see how expectations guide your decision-making, you may reconsider certain activities. You may decide to think twice before you say or act. When you fully understand your motives, know what you expect the outcome to be, you have space to adjust prior to the event, possibly eliminating some of the hurt or disappointment. If I had better managed my expectations when I pronounced my love so confidently, I might not have felt that initial sting and awkwardness.

Expectations can stifle energy. When you eliminate the expectation, people are free to move about as they need to without judgment attempting to guide the result.

To say that we will completely eliminate expectations entirely is not realistic. I have practiced consciously noticing expectations for years and I still have expectations show up every day. I regularly find myself expecting that I will have dinner, the sun will set and the moon will rise among other things. Expectations are, in and of themselves, not the problem. It is our attachment to what we expect should happen instead of being open to all possibilities. We get attached to the idea that he'll say he loves me back immediately in return. We get attached to seeing our kids so happy in gymnastics that they shower us with praise and thanks. When we practice recognizing those expectations, we better manage our responses when what we expected doesn't come to fruition. Or we change course ahead of time if a possible outcome is not something we are willing to accept.

It takes practice and a willingness to be conscious. As you tune in and notice your expectations, look at everything and anything. What are you expecting at work today? What are you expecting in 20 years? What did you expect when you got married/had a family? How can shifting your expectations change your experience of your days? When in meditation, ask yourself questions about how you experience expectations and how you work with expectations. See what comes up. Let yourself gain insight from the pictures that pop in. Keep in mind there is no right or wrong. This is for your information, for your growth. Let yourself see pictures, colors and images. As you move through what surfaces, take notes. Journal what you are seeing and learning.

Expectations play a part in our picture of healing as well. We are inundated with pictures as a society about what beauty, health, fame and success look like. We put pressure on ourselves to be something that ultimately may not be in our highest and best interest. We are always healing. Everything we are doing every day is a healing to ourselves and others. Our expectation is that the process be smooth, beautiful, easy and fast. The reality is that healing on the physical sometimes involves crying, hurt, pain, grief, illness and discomfort.

In order to experience complete healing, we must detach from any and all expectations of what that healing will look like. We have to be willing to suspend our expectations, all that we think we know, and allow spirit and energy to guide us. We have to operate from a space of complete neutrality and trust.

When I was pregnant with my first child, people often asked me what my birth plan was. While I didn't always articulate it well, I spent time meditating on and looking at the experience. I meditated on how I wanted things to unfold without getting too caught up in the details, without taking away the Universe's opportunity to guide me. I worked the space from neutrality and trust. I had enough wisdom to know that I didn't know it all. I had enough foresight to meditate on having the right team of people where I needed them when it was time. I knew that all I needed to do was trust and show up. I had to trust the process and that I would be ready to handle what unfolded. Meditation helped me manage the experience. It left me more exhausted than I knew possible and took far longer than expected. Yet, it was beautiful. Even when in mid-push my Mom paused to answer the phone (a friend was checking on me) instead of coaching me through, it all came together.

There is so much magic to behold when we suspend our expectations and trust the process. Meditation and working with intuition and energy is about trusting what unfolds. Healing happens when you aren't watching, when you aren't paying attention. You go to work upset about something your spouse said to you that morning and you come home with a new understanding of why they said it. All of a sudden your entire relationship changes. Where did the healing happen? How was it healed? You got what you needed, you heard the message, and you received the necessary information to see more clearly. When you open up to the messages, to what is unfolding in front of you and to letting go of what you thought or wanted or hoped for, what emerges is space for healing, for growth, for connection and for magic.

Meditation and energy work are tools that you can tap into every day, everywhere with no magic carpet requirement, no special attire needed, simply all that is needed is you, your neutrality, your willingness and your desire to practice, to see and to look beyond what meets the eye.

When you start exploring these topics, you embark on a journey that can last lifetimes. Reading and seeing energy, clairvoyance, is soul ability - it travels with you beyond this physical time, body and space. As you meditate from the center of your head, the place of curiosity and neutrality, you naturally create a space for growth. Some meditations may lead to great epiphanies while others might feel less enlightening. Rest assured, you are on the path to great self-discovery and awareness. The more you practice, the more you look, the more you stand to gain.

Any time something tugs at your curiosity, a question comes to mind, you see a peacock, you notice the sunset, you feel frustrated, happy, sleepy, look at the energy - ask yourself to see a picture. Disconnect from expectations and let yourself see from neutrality, to glimpse into your information and truths. Look at everything.

Opening up to seeing energy is sort of like doing a house project in an older home. You start fixing a leaky faucet which leads to replacing the cabinet which leads to painting the walls a new color and on and on until the entire house is redone when all you wanted to do was take care of one small thing. When you start looking, there is so much to see. There is always energy to notice, see, explore and question. Energy is always shifting and changing leading to new discoveries all the time.

As you practice, remember to validate your insights, big or small. Others might not always understand or get what you are attempting to do, see, create and that is okay. You can validate your own growth while also being open to finding and building up your tribe of people who do understand. Having a team to cheer you on helps. Make connections. Reach out. Share your experience with others and let others be part of your journey. See that there is a ripple effect between the different parts of our lives: when you focus on one part, other parts naturally shift. Allow the shifts to happen. Recognize growth in yourself and others. Be a cheerleader in your life and the lives of those around you.

Lastly, get out of your own way! How many times do we self-sabotage and mess ourselves up? When you open up to a spiritual path, trust what follows. This may be the most difficult part of such a journey: trust. Trust, trust, and then trust some more. Trust yourself, trust yourself and trust yourself again. Step back and get out of your own way by letting your intuition and clairvoyance be your guides. Trust that you have practiced and developed this ability. When you see or get an inclination, trust it. You have practiced and honed your ability through meditation, you have looked at your pictures, you know yourself and you have developed your language. Move ahead confidently. Imagine the free time that awaits when you no longer have to second guess yourself, worry or doubt.

We are all in this together. We are all connected in ways we may not directly see or know. We are all learning and growing separately but also together. Keep learning and growing. Continue looking and seeing. Let your curiosity guide you. Know that in showing up, in trusting in yourself, you are healing yourself and the world, one day at a time, one moment at a time, every day with energy.

The time is now to step into your amazing and awesome self. Get grounded, settle into the center of your head, create and destroy, surround yourself with your energy and let the pictures flow. See for yourself the energy of all you want to experience. If you see it, you can have it. You are powerful at manifesting. I am talking to you, yes, you! You, creating this life, this body, keep going! Keep seeing! Keep growing! I'll be right there with you - meditating, seeing, knowing and trusting energy every day.

CPSIA information can be obtained
at www.ICGtesting.com
Printed in the USA
BVHW040932131221
623912BV00017B/725

9 780578 308432